PATRICK AINLEY

G000024967

# BETRAYING A GENERATION

## How education is failing young people

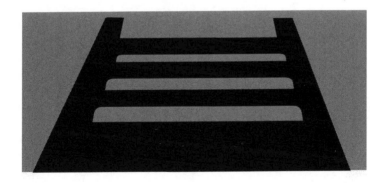

POLICY PRESS SHORTS INSIGHTS

First published in Great Britain in 2016 by

Policy Press
University of Bristol
1-9 Old Park Hill
Bristol
BS2 8BB
UK
+44 (0)117 954 5940
pp-info@bristol.ac.uk
www.policypress.co.uk

North America office:
Policy Press
c/o The University of Chicago Press
1427 East 60th Street
Chicago, IL 60637, USA
t: +1 773 702 7700
f: +1 773 702 9756
sales@press.uchicago.edu
www.press.uchicago.edu

© Policy Press 2016

British Library Cataloguing in Publication Data
A catalogue record for this book is available from the British Library.

Library of Congress Cataloging-in-Publication Data
A catalog record for this book has been requested.

ISBN 978 1 44733 211 4 (paperback)
ISBN 978 1 44733 213 8 (ePub)
ISBN 978 1 44733 214 5 (Mobi)

The rights of Patrick Ainley to be identified as the author of this work has been asserted by him in accordance with the Copyright, Designs and Patents Act 1988.

Cover design by Policy Press
Printed and bound in Great Britain by CMP, Poole
Policy Press uses environmentally responsible print partners

# Contents

# Acknowledgements

To Dr Martin Allen, who supplied many of the economic statistics and references in what was the first draft of this book, and who is now working on exposing the latest con trick being played on young people, their parents and the public by so-called 'apprenticeships' that are also detailed within, thanks largely to Martin's original research. (See *Another great training robbery or a real alternative for young people? Apprenticeships at the start of the 21st century*, rewritten and updated January 2016, available as a free download from www.radicaledbks. com)

# Introduction

At the end of 2015, the Equality and Human Rights Commission (EHRC) published a report, *Is Britain fairer?* Its answer was that in many respects it is not, and that it is young people in particular who are especially disadvantaged compared with previous generations. The report was greeted as 'The betrayal of a generation' by one national daily newspaper's front-page headline, which summarised the report as showing:

> Younger people have been hit by the greatest drop in income and employment in recent years compared with older age groups. They also face even greater barriers to achieving economic independence and success than they did five years ago. (*The Independent*, 14 November 2015)

The extraordinary fact that this book documents and explains is that this has happened despite the most extravagant promises of success and achievement offered to young people by extended education and training, boosted by access to an internet supposedly opening knowledge and information to all. 'Learn to succeed', 'Realise your goals', 'Achieve your ambitions', 'Be what you want to be', 'Make your dreams come true', 'Fly!' – these are the promises still made by educational advertising, amplified by mass media, and endorsed by every government. Starting earlier and going on for longer, education and training of all sorts continues to be promoted as the only road for individual aspiration in a world where all else is increasingly uncertain.

Unlike similar creeds, however, what Grubb and Lazerson in 2005 called the 'education gospel' is not a deliberate deception. Nor are many teachers conscious deceivers of those they teach. In fact, teachers are more deceived than deceiving. We feel uneasy about the too *great expectations* of education that we are asked to sustain. Many of our students are also increasingly sceptical, feeling that they are 'running up a down-escalator' (see Allen and Ainley, 2012), studying harder, but learning less, to become overqualified but underemployed. They put in more time, effort and money, but get less in return. This engenders a creeping loss of legitimacy that undermines learning at all levels, but which this book seeks to explain.

Much of the inspiration for the book comes from the epilogue that Pierre Bourdieu added to the English translation of his 1964 report with Jean-Claude Passeron on French students, that he called 'The bamboozling of a generation' (originally, *une génération abusée*). It concluded that the French education system at that time could not go on as it was without 'a showdown over the very foundations of the social order' (Bourdieu and Passeron, 1964, p 85). This occurred in May 1968, when students and workers took to the streets in what was nearly another French Revolution. Although a similar crisis of education is building in many countries today, it is doubtful that institutions will collapse as spectacularly as they then did in France. This is because modern societies have been thoroughly pedagogised.

As another French critic put it:

> Our societies present themselves as homogeneous, where the lively and common pace of the multiplication of commodities and exchanges has flattened the old class divisions and has engaged all in the same pleasures and liberties. Under such conditions, the representation of inequalities tends to work more and more as the model of academic ranking. (Ranciere, 2010, p 12)

It may seem extraordinary to readers in countries struggling to fulfil the millennial goal of getting all their children into primary school that, instead of the liberation it promises, education in developed countries forecloses possibilities. Indeed, basic literacy is a universal human right, vital in developed countries also. However, many early years teachers are aware that recent official approaches are hampering literacy learning. They are imposed by a regime of education that spends more on testing seven-year-olds than on books for them to read, and that then issues them with library tickets for libraries that have closed.

From primary to postgraduate schools, many teachers and lecturers sense the strange perversion of education with which they are forced to comply. They can only imagine creative alternatives to it. Hopefully, these will resonate with this book's account of how education got so blown out of all proportion to become a national obsession. In England, which this book treats as a case study or awful example to others, academic competition is generating anxiety, hysteria and stress among pupils/students and their parents alike. See Ken Jones 2016 for the larger context of education in the other nations of what is still the United Kingdom!

Like Jones, but unlike most books on the subject, the word education is not taken to mean just schools; it also includes colleges and universities. These institutions are set within the wider context of employment and training to appeal to all those who want a better system of education in the future, or who just want to understand the current bizarre situation. How this came about is the starting point for the book, but at the end I suggest some changes before more young people forsake any interest in learning critically from the past so as to move their lives forward into meaningful and productive adult futures.

## Outline of the book

Chapter One examines the postwar years in England when education expanded, schools became less selective and further and higher education opportunities increased. As the economy developed there were limited but growing opportunities for upward social mobility from the manual working class into expanding non-manual occupations and new professional careers. In a buoyant labour market, educational qualifications were only needed for these minority of positions. The chapter relates how the rise in staying on at school coincided with the changing nature of the economy, and in particular the decline of 'youth jobs' associated with industrial manufacturing. In response, successive governments encouraged and enabled young people to become more qualified. Their mantra was that a new global economy offered unprecedented opportunities for those who were educated but little for those who were not, as 'knowledge work' replaced the mass production associated with outmoded heavy industry.

This idea of the changing nature of employment is criticised in Chapter Two. It shows that increases in the level of qualifications are not being met by increases in employment opportunities, as more and more school, college and university leavers are overqualified but underemployed. According to the influential Organisation for Economic Co-operation and Development (OECD, 2015), for example, more than a fifth of British work roles require only primary-level education to carry them out. Other studies show large numbers of graduates unable to secure 'graduate jobs', as employer surveys repeatedly report many workers not required to use their knowledge and skills at work (see, for example, the latest UK Commission for Employment and Skills [UKCES] survey, 2015). These contradictions require a revision of widely accepted ideas about the occupational structure emerging in the 21st century.

This is the focus of Chapter Three, where it is seen that this emerging occupational structure has serious implications for both social mobility and social inequality, and has resulted in a great reversal of education policy (Allen and Ainley, 2013a). New divisions of knowledge and labour have followed from the latest applications of new technology to automate, casualise, deskill and outsource employment in the global economy. This is also recasting social class, breaking down the postwar manual/non-manual class pyramid at the same time as the gap between top and bottom has widened. This leaves the majority in a new middleworking class, or workingmiddle class, between – as has been said – 'the snobs' and 'the yobs'. The former, an internationalised top 1% or less (see Dorling, 2014), and the latter, an 'unskilled' – or 'rough' as compared to 'respectable' – section of the former industrial working class. This has been pushed down and 'chavified', as Jones put it in 2011, into a so-called 'underclass' status. As the class structure goes pear-shaped in this way, pupils and students in educational institutions of all sorts find themselves desperately running up a down-escalator of devalued qualifications. Yet education offers no way out, but functions to reinforce social differences through selection via exam results that are proxies for more or less expensively acquired cultural capital.

So Chapter Four argues that schooling has become primarily concerned with maintaining social order in the absence of wage incentives. Beyond containing the energies of youth, and far from representing a collective social activity, education merely confirms the advantaged starting point of a minority at the expense of a disadvantaged majority. Moreover, 'professional qualifications' supposedly guaranteeing access to secure employment are constantly degraded by qualification inflation at the same time as technical training is overtaken by technological advances. This employment situation contributes to the ongoing process of class reformation that serves to proletarianise the professions even as education promises to professionalise the proletariat.

Finally, Chapter Five looks to progressive responses to further changes in global production, potentiated by what Brynjolfsson and McAfee (2014) call a 'second machine age'. In the austerity conditions inflicted by the coalition government and its successor Conservative government in the UK, and on the Eurozone by the European Commission, both under the continuing dominance of finance capital (the banks), these latest applications of new technology produce further uncertainties and new inequalities. Along with other assumptions shared by all the austerity parties in the 2015 UK general election, and ignoring the gathering tsunami of climate instability, they completely discredit the current widely held faith in education leading to social mobility and employment to reveal a vacuum in social policy and a lack of economic and political imagination.

This is filled by concluding suggestions that point in a different direction by recognising the changed divisions of knowledge as well as of labour in society. These have implications not only for institutionalised learning (education and training), but also for politics and democracy. They imply the diffusion of general intelligence alongside the development of skills and knowledge in specialised expertise of all sorts. This involves resistance to a government and a state that is imposing the dystopian economic ideal of a self-adjusting market on society. The atomistic purposive rationality of this free market is destructive not only of human sociality, but also of the natural world on which humanity depends. It is therefore urgent that we learn from recent history to recover the purposes of education for human survival in the immediate future.

# ONE

# From jobs without education to education without jobs

So how did we get to this crisis point in education? This chapter provides an overview of educational developments in England since 1944, setting the scene to allow the magnitude of key social and economic changes to which education is expected to respond in the 21st century to be appreciated.

## The welfare state settlement

For nearly 30 years after 1945, the UK economy enjoyed a 'long boom'. Output increased, wages rose, and spending on the new welfare state increased accordingly. The Education Act 1944 established free state secondary schooling, albeit through a rigid tripartite system in which grammar, technical and secondary modern state schools were designed to channel the aptitudes and occupational destinies of young people from the ages of 11+. Corresponding as it did to the divisions of knowledge and labour in employment between non-manual 'middle' and skilled and unskilled manual 'working' classes, this left the 'upper' class private schools outside the state system altogether while still dominant over it.

The new state secondary provision was designed to match an industrial occupational order widely thought of as pyramid shaped, where, for example, in 1951 72% of employees were manual workers, with the majority categorised as no more than 'semi-skilled' (Callinicos and Harman, 1987, p 16). For these, the new secondary modern schools provided the minimal education needed for the factory floor. Technical schools equated with skilled or craft occupations. The grammar schools served as the avenue to white-collar/managerial work. They were also virtually the only way to progress to university, apart from through the fee-paying private schools with their close connections to the 'antique' universities of Oxford and Cambridge, notably through the exam boards. The 'upper classes' were thus largely absent from state schooling. Private schools catered for about 7% of the population, a figure not too dissimilar to today (although it is 14% in private sixth forms), and they are still closely connected with prestigious universities and even certain colleges within them. Their academic curriculum and character-forming ethos was mimicked by the grammar schools.

This left more of a binary than a tripartite system of state secondary schools, because technical education was expensive to provide and money was not forthcoming for it. So by the end of the 1960s, technical schools still only had around 5% of the secondary population, and only existed in about half of the local education authorities (LEAs). Instead, trade training through apprenticeships took place largely through day release from employment to further education (FE) colleges. Although the existence of different types of schools for different types of minds was also a feature of other European education systems, it took its most extreme form in England and Wales, where, in 1961, 73% of students left school at the age of 15 without any qualifications (Jones, 2003, p 46).

As education expanded, however, state schools became less selective, and in a growing economy there were more opportunities for upward social mobility, albeit limited mainly to the skilled or 'respectable' sections of the manual working class. Since it was harder for their daughters to pass the grammar school entry tests, which were weighted against girls to balance the genders, their sons moved in significant numbers into both non-manual, white-collar office and technical employment as well as into new and growing professional occupations. So it was soon being suggested that the tripartite model, with its psychological selection through what was later shown to be a phoney IQ test at age 11+ (Chitty, 2004), was not able to respond to the increased need for better qualified labour. To meet this demand, in 1963 the Robbins Report on higher education advocated more universities and higher technical colleges. The Labour Party, which had implemented the all-Party Education Act 1944 introducing the tripartite secondary school system, changed its policy in opposition, and after election in 1964 issued Circular 10/65 (DES, 1965). This invited, although it did not require, LEAs to publish plans to introduce non-selective comprehensive schools.

This was typical of the consensual politics of the original welfare state settlement between local and national authorities in 'a national education system locally administered' (see Ainley, 2001). The consensus extended to a 'mixed economy' of private and public provision in which state-owned nationalised industries sustained the remaining privately owned companies with the power, transport and infrastructure they required for their continued profitability. The logic of development was towards further public ownership and state support as British industry faced growing competition abroad. Like the public and private sectors, the 'two sides of industry' – employers and trade unions – were brought together to this end by the government as the third in this 'tripartite' administration of affairs.

'Planning' was not then the dirty word it became under Mrs Thatcher when everything was supposed to be left to the market (although lately strangely revived in a largely fictitious sense by George Osborne, Chancellor under the coalition and subsequently). In these circumstances, throughout the 1950s and 1960s, Keynesian 'demand management' of the national economy was able to maintain full employment, save in the 'depressed regions' of the North, Wales, Scotland and Northern Ireland (where in some Nationalist areas unemployment was never below a third).

## A golden age?

Complementing this general line of travel, after 1965 campaigners for educational reform joined economic modernisers in what was a genuinely popular and mass labour movement campaign for comprehensive secondary schooling. This allowed a 'progressive' approach to primary schooling, making it less about the selection of a few for the next stage and more about developing the abilities and talents of every child. The popularity of comprehensive reform – Mrs Thatcher as Education Minister described it in her *Memoires* as 'an unstoppable bandwagon' (quoted in Simon 1991, p 412) – made it difficult to reverse. Thus, John Major's promise of 'a grammar school in every town' helped to lose him the 1997 general election because electors knew that the corollary of selection to minority grammar schooling was relegation of the majority to secondary moderns.

Even so, state grammar schools survive to this day in 32 out of 353 local authorities – and some of them large ones, such as in the cities of Birmingham and Manchester (Trafford) and the counties of Kent and Essex. Reactionary politicians promise more of them as part of a fantasy politics in which they will miraculously restore 'the good old days' of upward social mobility (see Chapter Four for the latest developments). Another magic solution is the current consensus that 'apprenticeships' will similarly transform the UK's unregulated service economy into a productive German one.

Meanwhile, differentiation within schools and between autonomously competing schools, selecting parents via entry tests for their children, performs the same assortive function as tri- or rather bipartite schooling, but without the sharp cut-off point at 11+. Instead, students' journeys continue along various tracks to the new official parting of the ways at 18+, either to temporary work placements masquerading as 'apprenticeships', or as indebted under- and then postgraduate students.

Selection and competition are so intense nowadays between different brands and chains of supposedly specialist schools that it has been forgotten that most secondary state schools had become comprehensives by the end of the last century. In 1996, Caroline Benn and Clyde Chitty reported that 82.9% of pupils in England were in comprehensive schools compared with only 8.5% in 1965. Even so, educational research showed that children from families with a manual work background were less likely than their middle-class counterparts to succeed at school. This was both because of inferior economic conditions at home, and also because of 'language and culture', so that 'education alone could not compensate for society', as Bernstein acknowledged in 1970.

Nevertheless, many consider the move towards comprehensive schooling 'a golden age'. The ending of selection was accompanied by new curricular initiatives, often around English and the humanities. Yet many 'comprehensive' schools did not break with selective practices, continuing to 'stream' or at least 'set' for different subjects, while gender and 'race' segregation was only beginning to be challenged, let alone the inclusion of children with special educational needs and disabilities, which came later. Pedagogic innovation in what was taught and how it was learned was difficult, however, because curricular reform did not accompany structural reorganisation. So the comprehensive schools continued to be under pressure to match the performance of grammar and private schools in public examinations that remained based on traditional academic assessment. Many of the new curriculum initiatives that did happen, for example, were linked to teacher-assessed CSE mode 3 examinations. These did not enjoy the same status as GCE O-level for selection to specialised preparation for university entrance in sixth form or college.

It was also debateable whether all of those who progressed via the grammar schools to become what Lockwood (1958) referred to as 'the blackcoated worker' were really 'middle class', as it was then conceived. They were more an intermediate army of office clerks working in the sales and administration departments of the new large and bureaucratic corporations that developed in this period, or new 'white-collar proletarians' who, while being better qualified than manual workers, had only limited career and promotion prospects compared to management. It would therefore be an exaggeration to say that at this time the occupational order became less of a pyramid and more of a diamond shape, as more rose into the middle through upward social mobility, while corresponding numbers moved downward – they didn't.

In any case, even by 1979, manual workers still made up over 50% of all employees with only 16% in the office as opposed to the factory (Callinicos and Harman, 1987, p 14). The majority of 'ordinary' clerks were women who continued to earn less than skilled manual workers – witness the then ubiquitous typing pool. Both the growth and nature of white-collar work led to intensive debates on the left about the continued relevance of the Marxist conception of two opposed classes, a model that found it difficult to accept that any 'intermediate strata' could be anything other than 'transitional' between one side or the other. (These issues are considered in more detail in Chapter Three.)

## Limited absolute upward social mobility

In contemporary debates, 'social mobility' is always presumed to be upwards, and indeed, the limited upward social mobility of the postwar years was largely what sociologists call 'absolute', so that more people moved up, rather than being 'relative', so that, as the comparative inequalities between different classes declined, more people would also move down, allocated to their appropriate place via equal provision of education. This didn't happen because, as sociologist Ken Roberts explained:

> … during the twentieth century the middle class was growing in size, which in itself increased the likelihood of those born into the middle class remaining in this class…. Up to 1920 around three-quarters of sons born into the working class remained in that class. Amongst those born after 1950 it was just 50 per cent: the other 50 per cent had risen, at least into the intermediate class. (2011, p 186)

The consequence of this was that:

… by the 1950s a half of working class children were rising out of that class: typically one of the two children in a two child family. [Thus] Most working class parents in the second half of the twentieth century would have seen at least one of their children ascend at least to the intermediate classes. (Roberts, 2011, p 186)

This movement was sufficient to popularise the idea, deeply rooted in the respectable working class as much as in the traditional middle class, that education was a vehicle for self-improvement and aspiration. However, even in the mid-1970s, it was still the case that almost 40% of young people left school and moved into employment at the earliest opportunity. As Dan Finn noted (1987, p 43), it was not that the jobs available were particularly good – most were likely to be 'unskilled' or 'semi-skilled' – but with full employment and growing working-class affluence, education had little relevance to actual destinations, save in a minority of cases. Leaving school at 15 was therefore a rational choice for most, and involved a relatively straightforward transition to work without any of the 'vocational preparation for employability' – if not actual employment – now considered necessary.

There are classic sociological studies tracing the process through which young men followed their fathers into local industries such as mining. While many of these industries were already in terminal decline, there were many examples of towns dominated by particular employers where informal recruitment was more important than school performance. In these 'collective transitions', school friends often became workmates. As stated, it was predominantly boys who benefited from this process, as the first employment of most working-class girls was relatively short before they married and had children. This was still at a relatively young age, with the birth of the first child in the early twenties in the 1971 Census, compared with 30+ by 2011. With larger families than today, up to half of women stayed at home to look after their children, at least until their children started school. This compares with only one in ten stay-at-home mothers today – or 'housewives', as they used to be called.

The raising of the school leaving age (ROSLA) announced in 1972 was opposed by many working-class parents who saw it as a way of disguising rising unemployment, and it resulted in many 'reluctant learners' having to delay going to work. But while sociologists of education had long talked about anti-school cultures, or had described the difficulties in educating working-class students, Paul Willis (1977) provided an alternative understanding of the relationship between working-class boys in a 1970s secondary modern school and unskilled factory labour. He showed not only that the school taught them very little (if anything) that they didn't already know from relatives and friends, but that they saw it as an obstruction to their transition to work and to adulthood. For many 'typical girls', it was the same (see Griffin, 1985).

Collective transition to the workplace generally constituted the first stage of the wider transition from dependent child to independent adult. It was followed by transition from parental home to marital home, and then to being a parent, although for some young people this was far from straightforward, and could involve intermediate stays with relatives. This compared with earlier times when the process of transition from school to work and parental home to own home was even more 'condensed'. The welfare state nurtured this nuclear family-centred model (especially immediately after the Second World War, when women were returned from the factories and farms to ensure 'the adequate continuance of the British Race', as the Beveridge Report put it (HMSO, 1942, 52). Trade unions and employers shared with government a tripartite recognition of a 'family wage' to support a man's wife working part-time while bringing up their children. Sexist, racist and bureaucratic it may have been, but the welfare state worked.

In this context, many of the postwar industrial apprenticeships were denigrated as 'mere time serving', but their importance should not be underestimated. They were the closest that the UK came to emulating the German dual system of vocational training, bringing together employers and trade unions, again under tripartite arrangements facilitated by the government's Industrial Training Boards as part of an attempted industrial modernisation that was only finally disbanded in 1981. By 1950, 33% of boy and 8% of girl school leavers entered apprenticeships every year (Finn, 1987, p 55), and by the mid-1960s, up to a quarter of a million apprenticeships were on offer each year for school leavers, although by then only 6% of young women were apprentices (Mizen, 2004, p 51).

## Rising youth unemployment

Changes in labour market opportunities drove staying on at school, even beyond the mandatory requirement as that rose (from 14 to 15 after the Second World War to 16 in 1973 and on up to 18 in 2015 from 17 in 2013). The end of the 'long boom' and the economic downturn of the 1970s was initially registered by rising youth unemployment, as the first response of employers was to stop recruiting and to cut back on training. It then quickly became widely apparent that the new Youth Opportunities Programme (YOP) and the first one-year and then two-year Youth Training Schemes (YTS) were little more than what Finn (1987) called 'training without jobs'. Under the Department for Employment's (DfE) policy of 'counter-cyclical training', hopes were that trainees would 'hit the ground running' when the economy picked up again, but it didn't so they couldn't.

Following a national secondary school pupils' strike against YTS in 1985 and for an increase in the training allowance, young people voted with their feet. They opted to remain at school or went to college for new classroom-based courses such as business studies. From there, many eventually drifted up into the polytechnics that had been set up after 1965 alongside the existing and 'new' universities recommended by Robbins in 1963. Although participation in higher education rose from a mainly male minority of about 4% of 18- to 21-year- olds after the Second World War, towards 10% in the 1970s to include more women and older people, outwith the urban polytechnics, it was still largely restricted to what had become an institutionalised transition by traditionally middle-class young people from living at home to living away, as well as moving from school sixth form to work. As they used to say in first-year undergraduate sociology seminars, if you weren't middle class already, higher education made you so.

By the 1980s, more than half of 16-year-olds stayed on in full-time education for the first time, to reach 72.6% by 1993, when the number of 17-year-olds still at school or in college rose over a third, to 57.5% (Allen, 2004). Consequently, the nature of school sixth forms changed. Rather than being modelled on those of the grammar schools and public schools to 'build character', a 'new sixth form' emerged in the 1970s and 1980s. The curriculum that developed for the new generation of sixth formers was invariably a 'vocational' one. Despite this, comprehensive schools were blamed for rising youth unemployment by the last Old Labour Prime Minister, James Callaghan, who, in his 1976 Ruskin College speech accused them of not preparing their pupils for 'the world of work'.

After 1979 Thatcherite politicians routinely accused 'bog-standard comprehensives' of lowering standards, eventually to be counteracted by a National Curriculum and competition between schools for results in tests at ages 7, 11 and 14 introduced by the Education Reform Act 1988. By the time New Labour's decision to raise the age of participation in education and training to 17 was implemented by the coalition at the end of 2013, 70% of 16- to 18-year-olds were already recorded as being in full-time education, compared with only 5.9% in work-based training (Allen and Ainley, 2014, p 13). This level of participation would have been considered inconceivable at the time of Willis' study, as would the attainments achieved in the now unified GCSE exams at 16 and A-levels and other qualifications at 18.

A significant feature of youth unemployment in the last decades of the 20th century and on into the new millennium is that it has endured at a much higher level than the general unemployment rate. This was not the case earlier; in 1961, for example, out of a total unemployment figure of 330,000, only 10,000 were aged 15-19. In comparison, during the period between 1972 and 1977, when unemployment as a whole increased by 45%, the rate of youth unemployment for those under 20 increased by 120%. At the height of the 'Blair boom', for instance, half a million (10%) 18- to 24-year olds were unemployed compared with a 5% rate for the workforce as a whole, and the unemployment rate for 18- to 24-year-olds never fell below 20% of the total unemployed, despite the government's efforts (Bell and Blanchflower, 2009, pp 7-8).

Although accentuated by economic downturns, the decline in 'youth jobs' is part of a longer-term structural problem. Indeed, since 1981, when the Thatcher government repudiated the 1944 Employment Act's commitment to maintain full employment, unemployment has bottomed out at a more or less constant 2 million as monetarist economic policy controlled inflation by allowing the numbers of unemployed to grow whenever the economy was in danger of 'overheating'. (It is still around this figure today, although the size of the workforce has grown, as have numbers working part-time, making consistent comparison difficult.)

Youth unemployment has persisted ever since: in October 2014, when total unemployment had fallen to 1.97 million, equalling just over 6% of the economically active population and the largest annual fall in unemployment since records began, it remained at 16% for those in the 16-24 age group – nearly three times the adult rate. Exactly a year later, it was still 15.9%. Even based on the number of 18- to 24-year-olds 'not in full-time education' (the previous Office for National Statistics [ONS] totals having included full-time students looking for work), youth unemployment was 12%, double the general rate. For some minority groups and in some regions it was double that again. The high ratio of youth unemployment to adult unemployment is a feature of most developed economies, but it has been particularly persistent in the UK.

## From industrial economy to 'knowledge' economy

Rising youth unemployment and consequent staying on at school or college coincided with the decline of manufacturing, the importance of which in providing work for youth cannot be overestimated. Once the 'workshop of the world', as early as 1841 UK manufacturing employed over a third of all workers (Hobsbawm, 1968, p 121). Although it has continued to experience a long-term decline, even in

1979 heavy industry still made up 28% of total output and employed 26% of the total workforce. In 1964, for example, of 608,000 school leavers starting work, 425,000 were 15 years old, with 37% of boys and 35% of girls entering manufacturing (Finn, 1987, p 46).

Manufacturing industry was the backbone of the apprenticeship system, so its demise in the 1980s saw the numbers entering apprenticeships fall from 290,000 in 1975 to only 45,000 by 1996 (Ferri et al, 2003), most of them young women in the largest remaining apprenticeship – hairdressing. By the new millennium, manufacturing employed 12% of the total workforce, and by 2015 this had fallen to 8% (ONS Nomis database, see www.nomisweb.co.uk/). This was what was meant by a post-industrial economy.

Manufacturing declined most substantially in times of economic downturn – during Margaret Thatcher's first term of office, for example, when almost one in four manufacturing jobs disappeared. But between 1991 and 2001, when the City boomed and the housing market bubbled, a further 2 million more manufacturing jobs were lost. Even though there was an overall increase in manufactured goods, productivity growth enabled by automation and digitisation meant fewer people were employed to produce more.

UK manufacturing jobs were also lost overseas, especially to emerging economies – first to China, and then to countries where labour costs were even lower, for example, Vietnam and Cambodia. As significant, developments in technology, automation and computing, as well as the introduction of new management techniques of 'lean production', meant that productivity between 1998 and 2005 increased by 4-6% annually compared with 2-4% in the economy generally, according to accountants PricewaterhouseCoopers' 2009 report, *The future of UK manufacturing*. Indeed, labour productivity increased 50% between 1997-2007, this, on top of output increasing in 35 out of the past 50 years to reach an all-time high in 2007 (PwC, 2009). Even adjusted for inflation, the UK still has the world's sixth largest manufacturing output, with strong performances in certain key industries, for example, around a 15% global market share in Aerospace (mainly weapons manufacture).

The consequence of these increases in productivity is that the same, or more, output can be produced by fewer and fewer workers. And because the volume of consumer goods people need, or can be induced to buy, does not increase in the same proportion as their incomes, manufacturing employment will continue to decline even if the total output of the sector remains the same, or rises. In this sense, further growth of the service economy is inevitable, something apparently not understood by Conservative politicians determined to restore 'the march of the makers'. In fact, the UK economy – despite its current 'recovery' – still suffers from a comparative shortfall in new investment in manufacturing. Although, even if more investment were forthcoming, it would only increase productivity by making the sector more capital-intensive and more automated, thereby reducing the number of employees still further – as above.

When it first became clear that manufacturing employment was giving way to services, commentators looked to service employment to generate jobs requiring higher levels of skills and qualifications. For Leadbeater (2000), the number of 'knowledge workers' 'living on thin air' would replace people working on production lines performing relatively simple tasks. Likewise, for US management guru Peter Drucker (1993), knowledge workers would be employed to 'problem solve' in the 'thinking occupations' of the 21st century. Certainly, as manufacturing has declined and the economy has become less local and less parochial, educational qualifications are increasingly important in securing employment since they serve as indicators for employers who know little about the actual content of courses, but accept the accreditation given by educators, particularly prestigious ones such as the 'antique' universities. Rather than the informal collective transitions to traditional industries, recruitment to employment has been formalised. This only contributes to the renewed emphasis on officially sanctioned and institutionalised learning at all levels.

Meanwhile, 'the demands of employers', such as the former boss of the UK's largest private sector employer Tesco, Sir Terry Leahy, remain remarkably modest, with 'paperwork kept to a minimum and instructions simple', even as he lambasted a 'woeful' schools system that 'does not provide young people with the skills Britain's largest supermarket needs' (quoted in the *Daily Mail*, 14 October 2009)! Given such low expectations, it is perhaps not surprising that schooling continues to underperform despite the best efforts of teachers.

One in six people in the UK read below the level expected of an 11-year old – but then, Britain's top-selling newspaper *The Sun* is written for a reading age of 7! Similarly for numeracy, 'Almost a quarter of adults (24 per cent) in England scored level 1 or below, a higher proportion than the OECD average of 19 per cent', as recorded in an international survey of adult skills published by the Department for Business, Innovation and Skills (BIS, 2013, p 58). Although there are periodic 'literacy scares' occasioned by evidence that these rates are falling, they are more or less consistent with those recorded for national servicemen during the 1950s. Perhaps, however, given the depths plumbed by a mind-numbing mass culture marketed by corporate monopolies, it is testimony to the efforts of schools that popular understanding is not even lower and enduring levels of ignorance, prejudice and superstition are not even higher.

## 'Education, education, education...'

These developments provided the context for New Labour's 'standards agenda', the reforms to learning at the end of the 20th century that have been summarised elsewhere (see, for example, Ainley and Allen, 2010). Labour governments had previously emphasised ensuring full employment and a comprehensive welfare state 'safety net', but in the context of globalisation, postwar social democracy had to be re-thought and ways found to harness market forces to 'modernisation'. What Stuart Hall referred to in 2005 as Labour's 'double-shuffle' obscured the abandonment of gradual social democratic reform by espousing 'modernisation'. This meant adopting Thatcherism, but with some redistribution (see Hills et al, 2009). Much of this redistribution was funded on debt, for example, through private–public partnerships/ initiatives that paid for new schools and hospitals, but when the bubble burst in 2008, there was nowhere for New Labour to go.

After a slow start, education was one of the beneficiaries of New Labour largesse (see Hills et al, 2009). Education became the new economic policy, substituting for employment policy. This was left to international market forces as remaining Keynesian controls over the national economy were abandoned, along with direct control of the Bank of England. Thus, an enabling state would supposedly provide new opportunities for all, requiring universal 'upskilling' to take advantage of the new global opportunities. The approach had been signalled by the abolition of the old Department of Employment in 1995 and its subordination under the then much smaller Department for Education.

This augmented the centralised national system of education nationally administered that had replaced the previous national system locally administered. This was in line with the new public management increasingly imposed on the public sector since Prime Minister Edward Heath set up his 'competitiveness unit' to modernise the civil service. Quasi-autonomous non-governmental organisations (quangos), such as the DfE's Manpower Services Commission (MSC) (see Ainley and Corney, 1990), were established as independent agencies to contract out government services via competitive tendering for franchises that could include private sector companies. The MSC pioneered this new form of delivery with YTS.

Brokered by ubiquitous consultancy firms, up to half of the UK's public services are now 'delivered' in this way (Wilks, 2013), including many prisons and parts of the police service, as well as – increasingly – the NHS. Democratically controlled local authorities have been taken apart to hand over the services they once provided to charitable (and not so charitable) housing associations, private care providers and, of course chains of centrally state-funded academies and free schools (see Chapter Four). Independent of local authorities, these are supposedly more responsive to the market of parental demand. Like hospitals, autonomous schools, colleges and universities compete for parents-students/patients/'customers'. Competition supposedly 'drives up standards' policed by armies of inspectors checking the targets recorded by new technology.

The operating principle of this new market state is that power contracts to the centre as responsibility for delivery is contracted out to a workforce that is set targets according to the vagaries of the global economy. This was not an 'experiment' undertaken by the Thatcher government, as Andrew Fisher (2014) maintains, but a desperate response to an unresolved crisis of profitability, and one that therefore eventually and inevitably 'failed', despite New Labour's 'double-shuffle' mentioned above. It attempted to substitute for the falling rate of profit in productive investment by the commodification of services, opening up new areas for profitable enterprise.

As well as a new state form, the result is a new mixed economy in which public and private are no longer separate but complementary, as under the old settlement; instead, a semi-privatised state sector is indiscriminately mingled with and subordinated to a state-subsidised private sector. For instance, Michael Gove, as Secretary of State for Education, declared he had 'no objection to private firms running state schools for profit' (*The Independent*, 10 January 2013), and was angling for the inclusion of this proposal in the 2015 Conservative manifesto. His successor, Nicky Morgan, has so far ruled this out. (See Chapter Four for further comment.)

Instead of the state taking over the private sector, as was the tendency in the old mixed economy of the former welfare state, the direction of travel was reversed towards privatisation of the state sector by the state-subsidised private sector. This would also privatise politics, with politicians competing merely to offer technical solutions to the management of UK Plc. Even after investors' preference for more profitable financial speculation over less immediately profitable productive investment had resulted in the credit crunch, the only option of the coalition and then the Conservative government was to press on with their fundamentalist reform, using 'austerity' in the manner of Naomi Klein's 2007 *Shock doctrine* to inflict further dismantling and privatisation of the state. The European Central Bank imposed the same austerity to try to hold together the Eurozone, only pushing it towards disintegration.

It is central to the argument of this book that the vacuum left by the rapid unravelling of social institutions in a free market has been at least partly filled by 'education'. However, the education system cannot bear the weight of this expectation that has been put on it, and is therefore losing legitimacy at all levels. The policy response to this tends to be ... more education!

## And more education...

Well before New Labour's 1997 manifesto commitment to include half of 18- to 30-year-olds in higher education by 2010, governments had emphasised how changes in the world economy meant that opportunities for those who were highly educated had increased at the expense of those who were not. The 'new opportunities' that globalisation presented remained a central theme in New Labour education policy documents, beginning with the Department for Education and Employment (DfEE) 1997 White Paper, *Excellence in schools*, which promised to raise performance and 'standards' to boost 'the knowledge economy'.

A decade later, the New Labour government was still making the case for 'staying in education and training post-16', with a Department for Education and Skills (DfES) 2007 Green Paper claiming that a 25% decline in the amount of unskilled work since the mid-1980s meant 'it is no longer a sensible option for a young person to leave education for good at 16.' In the Foreword to a 2009 Cabinet Office White Paper, *New opportunities: Fair chances for the future*, despite the financial crash, then Prime Minister Gordon Brown proclaimed that the world economy would double in size, creating a billion new jobs for skilled workers.

New Labour's education reforms can be summarised briefly: all state schools were set challenging targets in line with national benchmark expectations, and required to confirm 'improvements' through the production of performance data and in regular Ofsted inspections. New Labour also proclaimed 'zero tolerance' of underperforming schools. For example, secondary schools achieving less than 30% A-C passes would be turned into academies, removed from local authority control, and funded directly by central government, or closed altogether.

New forms of performance management were imposed on teachers to 'remodel the teaching profession' as part of 'the schools workforce', not only altering employment conditions, but also producing tedious templates about the form and style of teaching that every lesson should follow. This has resulted in today's 'ticksheet of facts in a daily confinement of eight hours or more in an underfunded prison of partial knowledge' (letter to *The Independent*, 8 July 2014). Despite such critics, the proportion of young people passing 5 A–C GCSEs continued to rise to around 70% by the time Labour left office, with three-quarters of a million A-level entries.

As well as a more rigorous approach to raising academic standards, a raft of new qualifications was introduced as part of a 'vocational pathway'. The organisation and content of courses such as the General National Vocational Qualification (GNVQ) were said to reflect developments in the workplace, and therefore a more appropriate, but also a superior, form of learning to traditional academic study. According to Gilbert Jessup, for example, the new 'competence'-based vocational learning enabled all young people to reach their full potential by taking control of their own learning (Jessup, 1991).

Vocational pedagogy was justified by the way that standardised work on production lines, such as those pioneered by Henry Ford's mass production of motor cars, was being superseded by 'multi-skilling' enhanced by computerised technology. The emergence of this flexible post-Fordist way of working was accompanied by suggestions that in the workplaces of the future, semi-skilled production workers would be replaced by a new generation of computer-literate technicians, while management and authority structures would be more open and collaborative. Post-Fordist theories of the workplace can thus be seen as forerunners to arguments about the arrival of 'knowledge workers' in an 'information society' with a 'knowledge economy'. (For more on this, see the next chapter.)

But few of the thousands of new sixth formers who used BTECs (Business and Technology Education Council) and GNVQs as routes into higher education entered the 30 'top' Russell universities, let alone Oxbridge. On the contrary, they represented 'a business studies generation' (Allen, 2010), whose vocational qualifications never achieved 'parity of esteem' with academic qualifications. So, the 14-19 vocational diplomas introduced by New Labour were a complete flop (Allen and Ainley, 2008b), as those young people who were able to proceeded with traditional academic qualifications such as A-levels. These were originally designed in 1952 to prepare a small selected cohort for university entrance, and were only made more accessible through the Curriculum 2000 proposals involving 'modularisation' and the inclusion of new types of assessment.

This followed the merger in 1986 of GCE O-levels with the lower status CSE examinations to become the General Certificate of Secondary Education (GCSE). It contributed to the huge increase in attainment and staying on, especially by young women for whom qualifications were increasingly important as they, too, sought opportunities for independent careers. Finally, expanding higher education became a central New Labour objective. Started under the Tories, who doubled the number of university students overnight by merging polytechnics with universities in 1993, under Blair, participation rates increased to close to 40% of the cohort, despite simultaneously introducing undergraduate tuition fees of £1,000 per annum in 1998 (subsequently raised to £3,000 by the time Labour left office). Apprenticeships were also reinvented, first as John Major's 'Modern Apprenticeships', but later by the coalition/Conservatives, primarily as an alternative to higher education.

## Summary

This chapter has briefly described how, during the closing years of the 20th century, the relationship between young people and education changed markedly. From something largely irrelevant to most, education became much more significant for many. This did not mean that young people necessarily endorsed a 'love of learning' or developed an intrinsic attachment to 'education for its own sake' promoted by their teachers. Rather, having been 'pushed' into staying on at school and then going to college or university, they pursued educational qualifications in the absence of other alternatives (Wolf, 2011). While many young people have continued to be aspirational, 'acceptance' of school has also been a pragmatic response so that education is seen as important in allowing 'ordinary kids', as Phil Brown called them, and as they called themselves in 1987, to 'get on' with their lives and avoid 'falling down' the employment escalator.

This feeling of running faster just to stay still was clear from interviews with working-class – mostly black or Asian – students on an advanced level business studies course in the sixth form of a large urban comprehensive at the beginning of the 21st century. They wanted 'better than Sainsbury's jobs ... something to be proud of ... better position, better respect' (quoted in Allen, 2004, p 216). Similarly, 10 years later, university students asked,

> Just imagine if you chose not to go to university, then what would you do? Work full-time or even two part-time jobs, both for minimum wage, where you will just scrape-by and become trapped in a dead-end, demeaning job? Even then, there's no guarantee to get work so you might have to sign-on, getting a measly £56.80-a-week, forced to work any job no matter how dirty, embarrassing or dangerous, in fear of losing the benefits. (quoted in Ainley, 2014)

Although young people will continue to be curious and inquisitive about many areas of what they learn, while many teachers – despite the anti-educational environment of competitive assessment and control in which they find themselves – strive to make learning interesting, there is a difference between the 'value in use' and the 'value in exchange' of educational qualifications. Young people themselves are only too aware that the more qualifications they have, the better their chances of employment. All young people and their parents should therefore be seen as 'active choosers' (Ball et al, 2000), not just those who are 'middle class' or more privileged.

For instance, under very different economic conditions, the 'lads' in Willis' study (1977) and Griffin's 'typical girls' (1985) were also making active decisions, based on the knowledge they had about work and employment gained from their family and their peers. Facing an increasingly lengthy and uncertain transition to adulthood compared with the largely predictable and 'condensed' one in earlier periods, the educational decision-making of current generations of young people takes place in a very different context. The next two chapters examine the realities faced by young people moving into work in difficult times (Allen, 2015). Chapter Four then describes the fundamental shifts in education policy that have emerged as a result, before possible responses are presented in the concluding chapter.

# TWO

# New times

*[handwritten margin note: over qualified people doing these jobs.]*

The growth of the globalised economy has been accompanied by repeated official optimism. Governments throughout the developed world argue that if their countries are to achieve a high-value economy, then they need 'smart people'. A highly skilled workforce and therefore education, particularly higher education, must have the utmost priority. Thus, as noted in Chapter One, the UK's New Labour government emphasised 'education, education, education' for the new millennium. In contrast, Felstead and Green (2013, p 10) recorded 5.9 million jobs in the UK requiring no qualifications, but only about 1.5 million of those who were 'economically active' had no qualifications. 'At the other end of the spectrum', they added, 'while 8.2 million had a first or higher degree … only 6.8 million jobs stipulated that degrees were needed on entry.' Meanwhile, rather than major skills shortages, employers consistently reported large numbers of workers in the UKCES surveys not needing to use the skills and qualifications they possessed. This calls for rethinking the optimistic 'knowledge economy' prognosis.

*[handwritten margin note: not enough grad jobs.]*

## Fordism, post-Fordism or neo-Fordism?

Industrial manufacturing until late in the 20th century was founded on 'Fordism', a system of mass production, first implemented on a large scale in Henry Ford's car factory in Detroit in the US. Ford exploited advances in machine tools and gauging systems to make possible the moving or continuous assembly line, in which each assembler repeated a single task. Under Fordism, mass production was complemented by a new cheapened 'mass consumption' for the postwar working class – with sociologists Goldthorpe, Lockwood, Bechhofer and Platt (1969) descrying the emergence of 'affluent workers' in Ford's factory in Luton, where highly paid production line workers owned their own homes and took holidays abroad, for example.

The organisation and management of the workforce it required was as important as Ford's production line technology. Designed to destroy the independence of traditional craft workers, Fordist production was implemented through Frederick Taylor's 'scientific management' (1947). He aimed to improve economic efficiency and labour productivity by rigorous time management linked to a system of economic rewards for individual workers. For Taylor, as for Henry Ford, there was no basis for conflict between employer and employee if the former ensured the scientific management of production to maximise output.

The reality of working for Ford was shown by Beynon (1975), with production regulated by Draconian styles of management seeking to overrule stubborn opposition from the shop floor. For Marxist critic Harry Braverman (1974), the Fordism of monopoly capitalism continued to subordinate labour to capital in the way that Marx had revealed a hundred years earlier, but also to 'dehumanise' more and more work, as it spread from the factory floor to the office. Human intelligence and creativity was incorporated into the machinery, leaving operatives to work in a machine-like way, performing repetitively at a level of basic competence (Cooley, 1987).

For Marxist educationists Samuel Bowles and Herbert Gintis (1976), far from producing the creative and autonomous individuals that contemporary education theory claimed, in *Schooling in capitalist America* they showed that a 'correspondence' was maintained between education and the social relations of production. So schools with largely working-class populations mirrored the factory by imposing unquestioning subordination to authority and the importance of 'doing what you are told'. More selective institutions developed the 'independent' thinking required for managerial positions. This was like the 'correspondence' noted between the tripartite secondary state school system and the postwar tripartite occupational and class hierarchy in the UK. One of the questions asked in this book is whether in new times there is a new correspondence between education, the economy and social class, given that all three have been subject to ongoing transformations.

But just as, back in the day, Ford's workers fought back against the tyranny of the assembly line, as mentioned in Chapter One, Paul Willis (1977) documented the opposition of students who challenged schools to achieve the desired levels of conformity in the way that Bowles and Gintis (1976) implied that they did. Their struggle was self-defeating, however, as they only rebelled into the low-skill, dead-end factory jobs that they were probably among the last school leavers to walk into at 16, where, as Willis points out, they accepted their subordination as liberation.

Gillian Evans confronted the same cruel irony in our own time in her 2006 book, *Educational failure and working class white children in Britain*, only now at primary level. She asked how young men 'filled with pride about who they are … come to terms with the actual lowliness of their status' (p 11). And not only boys: it is 'a tragic indictment … that a child like Emma is likely to leave primary school unable to read and write proficiently' (p 45) because 'the whole of the school day … becomes a virtual battle … to inculcate in children a disposition towards formal learning' (p 83).

As the latest applications of new technology potentiated new forms of management that were pioneered in the private sector but then imported into the 'new public management' of remaining state-owned services, a new post-Fordist analysis emerged. According to the influential *Marxism Today* magazine in the 1980s, the crisis of Fordism was creating 'new times' with new opportunities for progressive politics in the 1990s. This was part of a more general crisis in capitalist society associated with and connected to the move from a labour process based on fragmentation and standardisation of work processes, to one that now required 'flexible specialisation' and 'multi-skilling'.

Post-Fordist analysis also emerged in education theory as Brown and Lauder (1992) suggested that because post-Fordist production replaced a small professional elite with a growing managerial service class, the potential for a new type of learning and curriculum was emerging, one that would develop 'collective intelligence' (p 27). Just as hierarchical Fordist enterprises would inevitably be replaced, 'top-down' bureaucratic schooling that assumed levels of intelligence were largely fixed would no longer be required.

As proposed in Chapter One, the 'new vocationalism' that emerged in schools and colleges from the 1980s on embodied 'post-Fordist pedagogy' (Allen, 2004). Yet, if the reorganisation of work along post-Fordist lines was seen as appropriate to some of the 'cutting-edge' sectors of the economy, especially in parts of the now increasingly capital-intensive manufacturing sector, there was limited evidence of its successful implementation on any significant scale. On the contrary, an intensified Fordism, or 'neo-Fordism', became evident in the fastest growing service sector, creating new work processes that now dominate many industries, whether publicly or privately owned.

## Fungible labour in a 'knowledge economy'

In his best-seller *Chavs*, Owen Jones (2011) describes the dismal experience of call centre employees, sitting in rows, 'reading through the same script again and again' while 'computers dictate the time and duration of breaks' (p 147). Employment in a call centre reflects what Brown, Lauder and Ashton (2011) termed a new 'digital Taylorism', making it possible to standardise and routinise what used to be more personal types of work. So, while the latest applications of new technology may raise the productivity of workers, at the same time they can reduce not only skill requirements but also the individual autonomy and job discretion that employees may have previously enjoyed. Call centres in the UK, for instance, now employ around 1 million people. The similarities between working on Henry Ford's early 20th-century assembly lines and labouring in the new service sector are even clearer in fast food chains employing thousands of 'operatives' in kitchens that have been turned into factories. The logic of remorseless profit squeezing is already automating this routinised labour as customers now touch screens to activate robotic cooking.

When management is in total control and no longer depends on the skills of the workforce that have been assimilated into the machinery, then individual workers can be interchanged or replaced easily, and also paid at minimum rates. Their jobs can also easily be automated. In this respect, the global army of fast food operatives are worse off than the generation of car workers who preceded them. Through relatively strong union organisation, the latter were able to enjoy greater security of tenure and benefit from collective agreements about working hours, holiday entitlements, bonus payments and overtime. Postwar car workers, for example, even if they were often temporarily 'laid off' when plants over-produced and vehicles stockpiled, did not suffer the imposition of zero-hours contracts, which are now a regular feature of 21st-century labour markets, one in four new jobs offered to the unemployed, according to Glassdoor Recruitment (Press Release, 20 August 2015).

Nearly three-quarters of a million people relied on zero-hours contracts as their main source of income, according to the ONS in September 2015. They include many in health and in education, where 35% of employers say they use them, especially in universities. Young workers and those over 50 are more likely to be on them. The continued existence of such Fordist (or 'neo-Fordist') working practices would suggest that at best, post-Fordism is an uneven development reflected in the growth of some occupations rather than others. As will be clear later, it is the more negative features associated with post-Fordism, such as the increased precarity of employment and the deskilling and de-unionisation of increasingly fungible labour, that have become more apparent.

In 1984 John Atkinson, at the Institute of Manpower Studies, wrote a prescient paper on manpower strategies for flexible organisations. He foresaw a workforce divided into an expanding periphery of individuals to be called on as required by 'a numerically stable core group that will conduct the organisation's key, firm-specific activities' (Atkinson, 1984, p 4). Only the core are 'full-time, permanent, career employees'. This 'core-periphery' model did not take off as immediately as Atkinson had predicted, but in today's ever more deregulated labour market, it is now coming into its own, potentiated by digitisation. So perhaps this is the new 'correspondence' that education finds with the economy through academic selection that appears to have nothing to do with anything save 'education for its own sake', but leads to intensifying competition for dwindling core employment. Meanwhile 'vocational relevance', supposedly closely related to the real conditions of employment, becomes increasingly irrelevant for peripheral workers.

This undermines arguments about the growth of 'knowledge workers' in a 'knowledge economy'. They are based on similar premises to those about post-Fordism, but emphasise the way in which 'knowledge' has succeeded traditional manual 'skills'. In an economy where practical 'knowing how' has made theoretical 'knowing what' academic, this type of 'tacit knowledge' has supposedly become 'the key factor of production'. This followed from the premises of human capital theory, first enunciated by Becker in 1964, but becoming conventional wisdom in the 1980s and 1990s with the idea that investing in the supply side of education and training would somehow create the demand for these knowledge workers to be 'employable' – even if there was no employment for them!

It was seriously proposed that this did not matter because of the shift away from traditional physical investment in machines, office equipment, buildings and vehicles towards intangible assets such as software, human and organisational capital, research and development, brand equity, design and copyright. This implied a huge expansion of education going on for longer in schools, colleges and universities, together with on-the-job training and continuing professional development in employment. Transition to the 'knowledge economy' was attributed to the mass application of computers across a wide range of jobs and the continued advance of specific developments in technology-intensive industries, and also due to the diffusion of general-purpose technologies across more traditional occupations such as retailing.

As with the post-Fordist thesis about changes in the organisation of production, it was claimed that the development of information technology enabled workers to take control over their work and facilitated the decentralisation of decision-making, making them more responsible and knowledgeable. However, knowledge was not distinguished from (bits of) information related together by a higher level mental ordering. Instead, muddled together, knowledge is often lost in and overwhelmed by information (Eliot, 1963). 'Knowledge' and 'skill' are also confused with their certification by qualifications that pass for knowledge and skills in much policy discourse.

## 'Lovely jobs' and 'lousy jobs'

Alongside high-skilled, knowledge-intensive employment there has been long-term growth of 'low-knowledge' (information processing), un- or semi-skilled manual jobs at the bottom of the service sector. As Sweet and Meiksins pointed out, in the US, 'there are at least three people heating frozen meat at McDonalds and similar workplaces for every IT expert' (2013, p 24). The increase in 'lovely' jobs – specialised occupations mainly in finance and business service industries located at the top end of the income scale – has been overtaken by what Goos and Manning (2003) referred to as 'lousy jobs'.

According to Goos and Manning (Table (IV, p 34), occupations growing between 1979-99 were headed by care assistants over software engineers, management consultants, business analysts and computer analysts and programmers. Educational and health assistants then figured before actors, entertainers, stage managers and producers, followed by treasurers and company financial managers. Goos and Manning also recorded large increases in the number of nursery nurses, hotel porters, merchandisers, window dressers and travel and flight attendants, among other low-paid service occupations.

The Institute for Public Policy Research (IPPR) (Cox and Davies, 2014) also conceded that the notion that future job opportunities would be concentrated in high-skill graduate positions had been 'overplayed'. It predicted that between 2012 and 2022, just over one-third of all jobs will be created in high-skilled occupations, with the remainder in medium and low-skilled occupations (Wilson et al, 2014). For example, while the number of health professionals is expected to grow by 1.6 million by 2022, an increase of almost 3 million care workers is also scheduled.

According to the Trades Union Congress (TUC) (Hudson, 2014), almost 80% of new jobs created since June 2010 were low-skilled, low-paid and often part-time, insecure jobs in sectors such as retailing, waitressing and residential care, with an average hourly wage of £7.95 or lower. As TUC General Secretary, Frances O'Grady, told *The Guardian* (5 September 2014), 'The economy is very good at creating low-paid jobs but not the well-paid ones that workers really need. Worryingly, the growth of low paid jobs is as much a feature of the recovery as it was the recession.' The TUC showed that only 1 in 40 new post-recession jobs has been full-time, with full-time employment representing only 62% of total employment, down from 64% in 2008, despite 1.3 million part-time workers preferring but unable to find full-time work – double that before the recession.

Of course, the Conservatives could claim during the 2015 general election that the increase in low-skilled and part-time jobs was not a permanent trend, but a reflection of an economy moving out of recession. However, Bank of England Governor Mark Carney had warned MPs on the House of Commons Treasury Select Committee that the UK's job market had changed permanently since the financial crisis, and that increased automation would add further to the number of low-skilled workers as well as keep wages down (reported in *The Guardian*, 25 August 2014).

## Under-skilled or over-qualified?

Against the Marxist correspondence theory of Bowles and Gintis referred to earlier, in which the function of mass education was to ensure that appropriate traits and attitudes were imparted to future generations of factory workers, what of the prognostication that a post-Fordist society could allow education to take on a progressive and liberating function, in the way that Brown and Lauder (above) had speculated? Such moves towards a 'high skill economy' would surely require the expansion of universities to augment the small community of scholars.

Marking 50 years since the publication of the Robbins' proposals, implemented as part of Harold Wilson's commitment to a new technological age with a new 'education escalator' lifting millions into white-collar jobs, Shadow Skills Minister Liam Byrne (2014) re-visited Robbins to emphasise the role of higher education. Particularly in relation to science and technology, he claimed 'classrooms of global citizens' (p 8) would participate in 'the knowledge-driven global economy' to secure Britain's position in 'the global skills race' alongside emerging economies like China and India. Yet, as Brown, Lauder and Ashton (2011, p 116) pointed out, there has been an 'education explosion in the supply of college educated workers in both affluent and emerging economies.' At the same time, the limited growth of high skilled/high knowledge jobs has been far exceeded by the number of university graduates now seeking them.

If this has been the case internationally, it has been particularly significant in the UK, where higher education has recently expanded rapidly. But then the 2008 credit crunch left a generation of graduates 'overqualified and underemployed', so that the 2013 ONS report, *Graduates in the UK labour market*, showed nearly half (47%) of new graduates unable to find a 'graduate role'. The Chartered Institute of Personnel Directors (CIPD) raised this to 59% in 2015. Examples of graduates in non-graduate occupations ('gringos', as Blenkinsopp and Scurry labelled them in 2007) are listed as receptionists, sales assistants, warehouse workers, cleaners, care workers and home carers.

The devaluation of qualifications has contributed to a situation where, rather than employers reporting serious 'skills shortages', significant numbers of employees were reported in successive UKCES surveys as not fully using their skills and knowledge in their current work roles, that is, they were 'overqualified'. As more jobs become 'graduatised' (Roberts, 2010, no pages), a degree is needed to 'get' the job if not to carry it out. As a consequence, 'graduates discover their qualifications do not guarantee middleclass jobs – merely admission to the pools that are allowed to compete for these jobs.'

## The self-employed society

Since post-Fordist knowledge employment allegedly increases autonomy at work, it requires 'high trust' and 'high discretion'. The enormous growth in self-employment has thus been seen as representing such new and positive changes. After all, many professions have always existed in this way, including GPs and architects in their private practices, not to mention the 'portfolio workers' of all sorts who are only as good as their last gig, while actors are notoriously never unemployed but only 'resting'.

According to the IPPR (Press Release, 14 August 2014), the UK had become Europe's 'self-employment capital' with self-employment a key driver of overall job growth as the working-age employment rate reached historically high levels in 2015. In *Self-employed workers in the UK*, the ONS recorded a total of 4.6 million self-employed workers, with an additional 356,000 people who were self-employed as a second job (ONS, 2014a). This figure can be compared with 1975, when only 8.7% (representing 1.9 million) of the workforce was self-employed.

This growth is celebrated by the Association of Independent Professionals and Self-Employed (IPSE), which announced that in the six years since 2008, the number of self-employed managers, directors and senior officials more than doubled to almost 240,000 (IPSE, 2014). Although representing less than a tenth of these, IPSE acts as a lobbying body, arguing on its web site that 'flexibility in the labour market is crucial to Britain's economic success' (http://www.ipse.co.uk/about-us). Self-employment has always been strong in the skilled trades, and IPSE records that these still represent a quarter of the total, with 167,000 building workers, 166,000 taxi drivers and 144,000 carpenters and joiners.

Self-employment, 'being your own boss', is a popular ideal. However, following Atkinson's 1984 model, it has been the more peripheral, badly paid and insecure parts of the labour market where self-employment has recently grown most rapidly. The average median income from self-employment in 2014 was only £207 a week, having fallen by 22% since 2008/09 (ONS, 2014a). This suggests self-employment is often a way of supplementing meagre income from elsewhere, and that many people have been forced to work for themselves, often part-time following redundancy from full-time jobs. Rather than a new generation of entrepreneurs, 'selling goods online' or 'odd-jobbing' is more likely to be the norm.

This partly explains why until recently the relatively high overall growth of the recovering UK economy did not lead to a corresponding rise in wages, which remained low despite falling unemployment. The number of new workers joining the labour force has increased, so that the size of the labour force is now at its highest ever. Media attention has focused on the numbers of European Union (EU) migrants and Syrian and other refugees arriving in the UK to seek work, and it is certainly the case that employers are able to recruit highly qualified workers from European countries for unskilled work.

In addition, the 24/7 service economy now provides part-time and weekend employment, and affords opportunities for women with children, not previously recorded as 'unemployed', to return to work. Employers often prefer people who are more 'mature' or 'reliable', and so want workers with 'experience'. This places young people in a familiar catch-22 situation of needing experience to get a job, but unable to get experience without employment, save through various forms of 'volunteering'. These range from school 'work experience' placements through to college simulations and graduate internships, as well as more or less coercive Department for Work and Pensions (DWP) 'direction' of the unemployed.

## Restructuring the labour market

Chapter One related how the declining opportunities for youth in the labour market was a major reason for young people remaining in full-time education, but from what has been described in this chapter, the growth of education and increases in qualifications have not improved their chances significantly. While youth unemployment, like unemployment generally, has fallen since the recession, young people are still finding it hard to enter the labour market, let alone get the jobs they want or that compensate them for their extended education. On the contrary, the New Policy Institute (NPI) found poverty for 14- to 24-year-olds had risen from 25% in 2003 to 31.5% a decade later, driven by low wages as well as high unemployment (NPI, 2015).

According to the ONS report, *Young people in the labour market* (2014b), young people who were in work, regardless of whether also in full-time education, were most likely to be working in 'elementary occupations' that include jobs such as kitchen/catering assistants and waitressing. The second most common occupational group that young people were working in was sales and customer services. By comparison, for people aged 25 to 64, the largest occupational group was professional occupations (22%), followed by associate professional and technical occupations (15%). It may therefore be that many graduates move out of peripheral occupations after a period (see the series of reports for the University of Warwick's Futuretrack by Elias and Purcell, 2006), but there are indications that the length of that period may be growing, so that more are trapped in what they initially thought were only temporary occupations.

Referring to the current cohort of young people as a 'lost generation' is unhelpful as well as inaccurate; this was why Martin Allen and I put a question mark after it in our book of that title (see Ainley and Allen, 2010). Instead, the term 'first generation' may be more appropriate to describe a cohort at the receiving end of changes to employment that – as suggested in Chapter Five – could be harbingers of 'a second machine age' with untold social implications, for education particularly. As it is, education already plays an important role in excluding young people from the labour market by 'warehousing' them for a lengthening period. At the end of 2015, more than 3 million – nearly half of all 18- to 24-year-olds – were in full-time education (and many more in varieties of part-time study or training), up from less than half this figure in 1984. This increase has occurred despite a falling youth population, even though the overall population of the UK has increased over the same period (ONS, 2014b).

It is not as if these developments have not been a long time coming, although they seem to have taken most commentators by surprise. As Ashton, Maguire and Spilsbury concluded in their authoritative 1990 study *Restructuring the labour market*, looking particularly at the implications for young people:

> Since our research began in the late 1970s, there has been a progressive transformation of the lower segments of the labour market as they have become dominated by insecure, casual, temporary and part-time jobs. As a result, the problem of unemployment is itself becoming transformed and incorporated into the everyday experience of a large section of the working class. (1990, p 203)

Five years earlier, the eminent German sociologist Claus Offe predicted that:

> For the foreseeable future labour markets in many countries will continue to exhibit a declining absorption potential, thus removing or excluding increasing numbers of potential workers [and] separating the employed and the non-employed. (1985, p 3)

## Summary

Having located the new situation of young people as consequent upon changes in the labour market occasioned by the latest applications of new technology, the next chapter concentrates on the transformation of the class structure that has followed from these changes in employment as they have worked themselves out in the UK in recent years. In particular, it addresses the vexed question of (upward) social mobility, which has already been seen to be the justification for so much recent education policy, and which knits together education, class and employment. It argues that the limited upward social mobility of the last century has given way to general downward social mobility in this one, and asks, what are the consequences for education?

# THREE

# Class structure in the 21st century

Social class officially no longer exists since former Prime Minister John Major announced the UK was 'a classless society'. His successor, Tony Blair, likewise declared, 'The class war is over', but he did not say who had won! Education has been central to contributing to the confusion that allows such assertions to be taken seriously. Since its inception in the 19th century, mass education held out twin promises of democracy and meritocracy. Both have been subverted ever since the ruling class ('the smallest ... best organised ... [and] most class conscious class', Roberts, 2001, Chapter 7) responded to the Great Reform Act by implementing mass elementary schooling to 'educate our masters' (Johnson, 1976), while maintaining its own elite schooling for the 'sons of the Empire'. Meritocracy, promising that applicants for any position would be judged solely on their abilities and qualifications, irrespective of social origins, could not be delivered save exceptionally in a capitalist, imperial and patriarchal society split between a minority employing class and a mass of employees, divided, in turn, by 'race' and gender, as well as by culture and (dis)ability etc. These are not social statuses but power relations.

Education is vital to maintaining that power. It impresses on the majority that it marks down for failure an apparently absolute judgement of their inferiority. As a student put it to me once, "If you let it, education really messes with your head." Psychological considerations also enter into the way in which, in an officially 'classless society', talking about education substitutes for discussion of class and the ways it has both changed and remained essentially the same over recent years. To draw a classically Freudian analogy, the return of this repressed content is manifested in hysterical symptoms that blow education up out of all proportion to its real significance. This chapter condenses the ongoing debates around different models of social class to get to the bottom of these confusions.

## Pyramid or diamond?

The postwar occupational structure remained pyramid-shaped – at least as most people thought of and largely accepted it. The subsequent steady growth of white-collar, managerial and professional employment led to claims, however, that society was becoming diamond-shaped as more moved into the middle from the top and bottom. In fact, this did not happen because, as already indicated in Chapter One, the limited social mobility that did occur was solely upward, with few moving down. Consequently there was a long-term decline in the size of the manual working class, from well over two-thirds of employees in 1951 who were still manual workers to just over half by 1979 (see Todd, 2014). The non-manual working middle class of employees expanded proportionately.

Between 1991 and 1997 alone, the number of administrative and managerial workers increased from 17.5% to 18.7% of the working population, and professional and technical workers from 19.5% to 21% (Allen, 2004, based on Rose and O'Reilly, 1997). Maybe this was why Labour's deputy leader, John Prescott, proclaimed before the 1997 general election that "we are all middle-class now." If he was right, there would be major implications for Labour as 'the party of the working class'. As also noted in Chapter One, the growth of white-collar workers had stimulated a debate among sociologists about whether this new stratum really represented a 'new middle class'. If this were so, it would refute Marxist predictions that class relations would become increasingly 'polarised' as the working class grew, leaving many at the bottom against a few at the top, with none in between.

Marxist writers, particularly Harry Braverman (1974) in the US, continued to restate the 'proletarianisation' thesis, noting that although the number of clerical workers had expanded rapidly, their skill requirements were being seriously reduced, alongside their career and promotion prospects. As Crompton and Jones (1984) in the UK added, the fact that white-collar work was dominated by women meant that promotion prospects were reduced further. For others, however, the growth of 'intermediate' groups constituted a major challenge to the Marxist model. Roberts et al (1977) saw a 'fragmentary class structure', while Olin Wright, in his *Debate on classes* (1989), augmented the two main Marxist classes of employers and employees, as well as Marx's self-employed 'petty bourgeoisie', with eight other 'class locations' that could be identified according to the different 'productive assets' they possessed.

Wright sought to integrate Marx with Weber who had argued that in addition to the divisions based on ownership or non-ownership of capital, class divisions were also the product of different 'marketable skills' possessed by individuals. This resulted in a multiplicity of classes or statuses, particularly around the middle. Another complication was Wright's development of the 'moratorium' idea that lengthening education imposed on young people; during this time he suggested they were effectively removed from the labour market and consequently any class allocation.

## Or an hourglass with a squeezed middle?

At the beginning of the 21st century, the 'middle' continues to be the focus of attention. The context is very different, however, with Goos and Manning (2003, p 2) proposing that the drift towards either 'lovely' or 'lousy' jobs has been at the expense of those in the middle. This 'hollowing out of the middle' has, they say, followed the increasing use of computer technology that, together with outsourcing and downsizing, has allowed the automation of more and more 'routine' jobs.

The use of labour-saving machinery in the office in particular is not new. Following the deskilling of manual craft labour, Braverman (1974) described the effects of what can now be recognised as the first wave of technological change occasioned by computing, particularly affecting those jobs associated with data-processing. Braverman showed how these developments led to the deskilling and laying off of established clerical occupations such as book-keeping, which he contended was becoming a 'mechanical operation' (p 338). Zuboff later but also presciently detailed similar effects on bank tellers and others, *In the age of the smart machine* (1988).

Forty years on, in what Brynjolfsson and McAfee (2014) call the 'second machine age', the deskilling of labour gives way to its substitution. Nowhere is this more apparent than in financial services, as banks close hundreds of branches, making thousands redundant. With personalised banking now based on laptops and mobile phones, customers no longer spend lunchtimes queuing for a counter clerk to perform relatively routine transactions on their behalf. More general accountancy is going the same way, with computer packages allowing individuals to file their own tax returns while maintaining their own records. Surveillance also plays a part, obviating parking wardens and much policing, for instance, while the taxi app Uber threatens black cab drivers more than geodesic mapping. Uber illustrates, too, how easily these app-based businesses are set up, using the self-employed who contract into them to supply services on demand. Similar web businesses for job finding and provision of services proliferate with little extraneous support. Online shopping also affects the high street as even payday loan and betting shops go online, presenting new problems of regulation.

University of Oxford researchers Carl Frey and Michael Osborne estimated about 47% of current US employment is at risk 'perhaps over the next decade or two', and that 'sophisticated algorithms could substitute for approximately 140 million full-time knowledge workers worldwide' (2013, p 4). For the UK, they predict 35% of all jobs at risk in 10 to 20 years because of automation, although initially it will be relatively low-skilled routine employment in office and administrative work that will be most affected, but soon 'involving everything from legal writing, truck driving and medical diagnoses, to persuading and selling' (2013, p 4).

How this affects social class was discussed in The Work Foundation's *The hourglass and the escalator* (Sissons, 2011), which, like Goos and Manning, endorses 'the hollowing out' idea, 'increasing polarisation in the labour market':

> During the recession, and the seven years before it, occupations which have lost the largest number of jobs tend to be in middle-wage routine manual and non-manual occupations. For men this has meant the loss of significant numbers of jobs in process, plant and machine operative occupations; for women it has meant large-scale reductions in the numbers working in administrative and clerical occupations. (Sisson, 2011, p 30)

While, as the UKCES data show, there are still over 3.5 million 'administrative and secretarial' workers, along with another 3.5 million employed in 'skilled trades', the decline in traditional 'middling jobs' has implications for the pyramid model of social class, and still more for the optimistic prognosis of it being transformed into a diamond. Instead, it is now widely proposed that an 'hourglass' occupational structure has emerged.

The 'hollowing out of the middle', especially traditional clerical and skilled manual jobs, has, according to the hourglass idea, been compensated for by a growing demand for traditional managers and professionals and new 'higher middle' designers and technicians, as well as a new group of 'para-professionals'. In other words, the hourglass is essentially symmetrical, with high-level skilled employment in the top half matched by low-level unskilled employment in the bottom, with a pinch-point in between blocking any upward social mobility. Such a picture is illustrated in the University Alliance's prediction of *The way we'll work: Labour market trends and preparing for the hourglass*

(2012, p 8). This emphasises the increased importance of graduates in the labour market, and therefore the continued need for investment in the university sector, as opposed to lower-level vocational training such as apprenticeships designed for 'middling' jobs that increasingly no longer exist. It suggests a 'new correspondence' between education and the economy, in which a degree is needed to remain in or reach the top half of the hour glass.

The Alliance, which represents 'non-elite' universities reliant even more than most higher education institutions on the continued expansion of student numbers, seeks to dispel concerns, outlined in Chapter Two, that there is a glut of graduates compared to the limited number of 'graduate jobs' leading to degree devaluation.

> Just as popular opinion holds that we have too many graduates, there is a widely held assumption that we need more apprentices in the UK but this should also be tested against evidence provided by future labour market projections. At present, the quality of and benefits from apprenticeships vary greatly. The Government needs to consider how limited public investment can be most effectively targeted considering the reduced employment share for this group of occupations in the UK. (University Alliance, 2012, p 4)

UKCES also predicts a continuing increase in the number of 'managers, directors and senior officials' by 18% from 1992 to 2020, along with the number of 'professionals' by 19%, and a 14% increase in the 'associate professional and technical' group. Employment has grown most rapidly for associate professionals engaged in culture, media and sports occupations, together with health and social care (UKCES, 2015, p 83). If the 'associate professional' category is included, over 40% of jobs could be considered to be in the 'lovely' jobs category in the upper half of the hourglass.

## Instead, the class structure goes 'pear-shaped'

However, the validity of the hourglass model depends on the nature of many of the new jobs that have been created, particularly for occupations considered to be 'para-professional'. This type of employment has grown at the expense of traditional professions that have been 'bite-sized' by being broken down into detailed tasks. This process may be presented as 'multi-skilling' if applied across a wider range of activities by 'multi-tasking'. In other cases, these are merely serially repetitive operations, reducing professions to the condition of wage labour, that is, proletarianising or deprofessionalising them. This repeats Braverman's version of what happened to skilled manual work as new technology was applied to deskill and automate it from the 1970s onwards, but moves the process up the employment hierarchy. The same effects are then replicated at professional and managerial level, as Zuboff previously showed in technical and clerical non-manual occupations.

What the government now calls 'the schools workforce' can be taken as an example of what was, until recently, one of the fastest growing areas of employment. Alongside full-time equivalent teachers rising from 405,800 in 2000 to their peak of 442,000 in 2012 (falling to around 440,000 today), DfE figures show a threefold increase in teaching assistants from 79,000 to 232,300 over the same period. As the number of teaching assistants has increased, specific qualifications, notably two-year foundation degrees, have been developed to 'professionalise' this occupation. Such qualifications may, of course, act as a ladder towards full certification as a teacher, but there is also the danger of being stuck at that level or laid off when cuts are made.

Regular conditions of employment are less secure for teaching assistants, with 87% of respondents to UNISON's 2014 survey of its teaching assistant members only paid during term times, while two-thirds complained about the excessive amount of 'cover' they did for absent teachers. Others commented that extensive time dealing with pupil 'behavioural issues' limited their opportunities to assist children with learning, that they were not included in staff training, and that they felt isolated; 83% expressed concern about working unpaid hours, with nearly a third being 'very concerned' about this; 56% said they regularly worked unpaid hours – more than a third of these working four or more hours unpaid extra per week; and 12% of respondents worked more than six hours of unpaid overtime every week.

Many commented on working through lunch unpaid, assisting with school trips without pay for the extra time given, and having to undertake training in their own time. Nevertheless, most of those surveyed considered that they did valuable and educationally useful work, but were not adequately remunerated for it, 95% expressing concerns about low pay. Where they are employed by local authorities and paid according to the local government pay spine, the minimum starting salary for a teaching assistant is £12,145 and the maximum £17,802, although a high-level teaching assistant at foundation degree level can expect slightly more. In comparison, the average gross salary for all full-time qualified teachers working in state schools remains £37,600 under a public sector pay freeze, allowing 1% increases at most.

Debate about such para-professional work is often focused not only on the autonomy and discretion supposedly exercised in better-paid professionally regulated employment, but also on the vexed nature of 'skill'. This has been largely redefined into its component competences with which skill has been confused, particularly whether the competences collected together in 'multi-skilling' are recognised as amounting to more or less than those integrated in a holistic skill that constitutes more than the sum of its component parts (Ainley, 1993). Skill, in this *gestaltic* sense, cannot exist without knowledge, their integration being recognised as 'expertise' (Collins and Evans, 2007, and again as Collins, 2014). So-called 'personal and transferable skills' can then be seen as no more than the generic competences required in nearly all employment and many other social situations – to use new technology alongside the 'soft skills' of interpersonal relations, for instance. These also tend to be the listed competences that constitute the 'employability skills' which, in the absence of employment, are made so much of at all stages of 'the student journey'.

Such redesignations as skilled and knowledgeable, multi-skilled or merely competent affect the occupational order, which, as Parkin affirmed, is the basis of the class structure (1972, p 18). Levels of pay then provide the main indication of a person's 'market situation' in terms of their worth. Here, arguments for the hourglass society run into trouble because income data show less of an hourglass and more of a pear. According to the Hills report (2010), there is not the clumping of income around the top 30-40% of the incomes ladder that an hourglass structure would indicate. Instead, after high returns to the top 5%, weekly earnings tail off gradually, producing a situation where the majority of the population remain in a relatively narrow income band near the base of what is a pear-shaped distribution. Standing at £35,600 for the top 20%, average income falls sharply to £27,900 for the top 30%, but only to £23,100 for the top 40% compared with £16,500 for the bottom 40%.

Income data emphasises sharper differentiation at the top. Both the 2010 Hills report on economic inequality in the UK and Inland Revenue percentile returns show that really high levels of income are restricted to 1%, or at most, 2% of earners – more like a shard than anything else. According to the Equality Trust in 2011, the top 1% of earners had an average income of £248,480, but within that, the top 0.1% had an average income of £922,433 (see also Dorling, 2014). According to Lansley (2012), the number of UK citizens with incomes over £1 million rose eightfold in the 10 years before 2006, so that today's wealthiest citizens have now acquired shares of income equivalent to those their counterparts enjoyed 80 years ago. Top UK directors, for instance, earn 120 times the average wage, up from 45 times in 1998. Even more extreme inequalities of income exist in the US.

The most comprehensive international data on this has been provided by the influential Thomas Piketty (2014), who connects inequalities in income to much larger inequalities in wealth. Piketty shows that when the rate of return on capital exceeds the rate of growth of output and income, consequent on a 'wages squeeze', growing inequalities in income and wealth inevitably emerge. Piketty's data for the UK adds that, after falling significantly between 1910 and 1970, the proportion of wealth owned by the top percentile is now approaching 40%, and for the top 10% it is 70% (Picketty, 2014, p 344). All boats are not therefore rising along with the wealthiest. Nor, to put it another way, is their wealth 'trickling down'.

## So farewell to the middle class?

Instead, with the contraction of core employment, there is no floor for the next tier down of managers and administrators to stand on. Or at least, the secure floor – or 'glass ceiling', as it presents itself to those below trying to break through it – has moved several stories up. As it continues to rise, it affects the children of the old managerial and professional middle class, less of who can take their place in the pecking order for granted. Like those below them who could formerly have hoped to rise from the aspiring and usually skilled formerly manually working class, they are goaded into running faster up the down-escalator of general downward social mobility. All have to compete for the dwindling core of secure and well-paid positions, or else fall into the growing and insecure periphery of employment. As McCullough (2015) writes, 'Previous middle-class certainties have collapsed.'

If there has been a fall in numbers of 'middling' jobs, then, rather than income differences being hourglass-shaped, the middle 20% of earners are spread across a comparatively narrow income band. This coincides with the shape of the Hills report's income curves, and it implies that income inequalities are producing a pear-shaped class structure as a result of this general 'pushing down' of income levels at the same time as there is heightened polarisation away from the mean by those at the top – a tear-drop more than a pear, perhaps, or a shard with a big base!

Indications that since the recession the pushing down of wages is not just restricted to those in 'lousy jobs' came from a *Daily Telegraph* report (15 June 2012) concerned that 'middle-class' employees had experienced some of the largest falls in earnings and the biggest fall in their standard of living since 1981. Although it blamed 'rising taxes', the article confirmed Institute for Fiscal Studies (IFS) findings showing those earning the equivalent of more than £47,000 had seen their pay fall by 5.15%, while those earning less than £10,000 had lost out by only 1%.

The growing trend towards more low-paid employment was noted in Chapter Two, where it was related to automation with increases in particular types of jobs and to new styles of management and work organisation, especially, as above, again following Atkinson's model of contracting out from a contracting (in size) core to a growing periphery. This chapter now develops the widely held view that there has been a relative decline in pay levels in the UK for all except a small minority at the top, but suggests that this is the result of wider social and political factors as much as it arises from the latest applications of new technology.

Lansley (2012) alleged that in the UK (as well as in the US), the squeezing of middle incomes, but also the increased impoverishment of those at the bottom, have followed from the policies of centre-right governments prioritising reducing inflation over promoting growth. The Cameron-Osborne 'austerity plan' intensified these trends until a partial recovery was engineered as the 2015 general election approached. In the US, the mild reflationary policies of the Obama administration created higher rates of growth and many more jobs earlier in the cycle, but wage increases are also yet to return to pre-downturn levels. President Obama regards as 'the defining challenge of our time ... a dangerous and growing inequality and lack of social mobility that has jeopardised middle-class America's basic bargain that if you work hard you've got a chance to get ahead'.[1]

The UK equivalent is what Ed Miliband called 'the British promise' that every generation will be better off than their parents (in a speech to parents in Gateshead, 4 February 2011). In his 29 March 2015 speech promising undergraduate fee reductions in the run-up to the 2015 general election, he promoted the measure as avoiding 'a disaster for

---

[1] www.whitehouse.gov/the-press-office/2013/12/04/remarks-president-economic-mobility

the future of Britain' because 'a country where the next generation is doing worse than their parents is the definition of a country in decline'. For the first time, it looks as if this 'British promise' will not be fulfilled due primarily to an intractable economic crisis aggravated by climate as well as demographic change (fewer in the younger generations to care for more in the older generation who are also living longer), especially if – as the pear-shaped class structure implies – the limited upward social mobility of the last century has given way to general downward social mobility in this one.

The shift towards much greater income inequality in the 21st century, however, is a more fundamental one, going well beyond the situation in particular countries. As asserted in Chapter Two, it resulted from capitalism's need to reverse a major 'profits squeeze' in the 1970s (Glyn and Sutcliffe, 1972), and to resolve what Andrew Glyn (2006, p 7) referred to as a 'distributional struggle' between labour and capital over wages and profits. As Glyn's work emphasises, rather than seeing economic development as a linear process, or as mainstream 'neo-classical' economic theory implies, a constant readjustment of incomes to productivity, the economy should be seen as comprising competing social groups or classes where the fundamental problem is one of 'distribution', not neo-classical 'efficiency' (with thanks to Martin Allen for this concise summary).

Approaching economics in this way was always fundamental to the political economy practiced by the founders of the discipline, such as Adam Smith and David Ricardo, and which, of course, continued to be central to Marx's *Capital* (1971). In contrast to neo-classical economics, which explains the overall levels of wages but also differences between the wages of particular groups of workers as the result of differences in 'marginal productivity' – and in this respect, UK workers are often said to lack the productivity of their international competitors – the distribution of rewards reflects the relative economic and social power of those who receive them.

Thus, as Picketty states, the huge income of chief executive officers, or 'super managers', is a reflection of their ability to determine their own salary and bonus levels, not an accurate measure of their individual contribution to increased output and productivity. It is a consequence of the dominance of private monopoly financial capital over state capital and productive capital in the UK since 1979, with the semi-privatised state sector subservient to the state-subsidised private sector in the 'new market state'. When private and state capital shared in the administration of the former national welfare state, the long boom of the postwar period had brought both rising wages and full employment.

Until the 1970s unemployment never rose above 1 million, and was high only, as mentioned in Chapter One, in the 'depressed regions'. However, the increasing power of organised labour resulted not only in growing industrial conflict and upward trends in inflation, but more fundamentally, in the squeeze on levels of profitability noted above – not helped by the sharp rise in oil prices. For Lansley, because wage earners shared more or less equally in the rising postwar prosperity until the 1973 oil crisis, this ensured that demand was maintained to guarantee continued economic growth. As the power of organised labour declined, Lansley shows wages fell and profits surged.

If potential profits were restored – the proportionate income share going to labour having fallen from 65% in the 1970s to 55% by 2010, with corporate profits up from 13% to 21% (Fisher, 2014, p 39) – they also had to be *realised*. As a result, increased supplies of credit have been needed to provide the spending power no longer generated by wages. Thus, in the early years of the 21st century, personal debt in the UK had soared to well over 150% of GDP. Pre-Christmas 2014 alone, Britons ran up more than £1.25 billion on credit cards, loans and overdrafts (*The Guardian*, 3 January 2015). Yet it is the figures for public debt, which are much lower in comparison, that continue to be the main obsession for government. Additionally, the loss of tax revenues, which are a consequence of low levels of wages, intensified the difficulties the coalition government had with closing the annual deficit, still forecast to be around 5% of gross domestic product (GDP).

## Or farewell to the working class and hello to the precariat?

Not only has the restoration of profit levels depended on austerity, privatisation and attacks on trade unions, it has also been strengthened by increased deregulation of the labour market with the casualisation of more and more employment, for example, with the expansion of zero-hours contracts. Once again, the policies implemented in the UK and US have been the clearest examples of this.

Marx coined the term 'reserve army of labour' (RAL) to describe how the unemployed or underemployed sections of the working class were essential to the cycle of capitalist production as it alternated through periods of boom and bust. It was during periods of crisis that this RAL was reconstituted, ratcheting up to include 2 million estimated above as permanently unemployed at any one time since the 1980s. As Clark and Heath (2015) recall, 'The pattern of cycling between low-paid work and unemployment was evident at the time of the UK's last recession' [in the early 1990s] (note 60, p 258). However, contrary to the impression given in the mass media, very few of this so-called 'underclass' are the same people plunged permanently into a 'culture of poverty'; rather, as Shildrick et al (2010) found in Glasgow and Teesside, most churn through part-time, insecure and low-paid jobs intermitted by spells of unemployment.

The return of such a RAL might have been considered inconceivable in developed economies during the 'affluence' of the postwar years, although it continued to grow in the 'third world', post-colonial countries. But a growing zero-hours peripheral labour force in the heartlands of the capital shows the RAL is back with a vengeance. In particular, the marginalisation of young people from the labour market, which, as Wright remarked, is reflected by a prolonged stay in the holding pens of full-time education or training, would suggest that young people now contribute a significant part of this reconstituted RAL (Ainley, 2013).

As capitalism developed, Marx asserted that the proletariat as a whole would experience an increased class consciousness, a growing social awareness not only of their common impoverishment, but also of the nature of their exploitation at the hands of capitalists. One argument to the contrary pointed to the subversive effect on organised workers of the 'underclass' – Marx's *lumpenproletariat*, 'that passively rotting social scum', as he described them in 'The communist manifesto'. Debate about the formation of an 'underclass' has perhaps therefore been dominated by right-wing think-tanks, such as the Institute of Economic Affairs in England, and neo-Conservative intellectuals from the US such as Charles Murray, whose claim to find an 'emerging British underclass' featured prominently in *The Sunday Times* magazine (26/11/89) and was subsequently published as a book by the Institute of Economic Affairs.

Such right-wing accounts emphasise the moral and individual (if not genetic) shortcomings of those 'trapped' on benefits. These, it is argued, have resulted in their continued marginalisation in a 'culture of poverty' leading to loss of any work ethic. The 'not-hard working class' are then constantly implicitly and explicitly demonised by pro-austerity politicians in contrast with the 'hard working people' they claim to represent. Labour substituted this most overused of all phrases in the 2015 general election campaign for the traditional 'working class', while for the Conservatives it represented the respectable middle working/working middle to whom they appealed.

Following from the extent of low pay and the huge number of 'zero-hours' workers described in Chapter Two, just a quarter of whom work a full-time week and who on average earn nearly £300 a week less than those on full-time contracts, the TUC has announced that a 'two-tier' workforce is emerging, with many people part of a new working poor (TUC, Press Release, 15 December 2014). Yet 30 years earlier, and seeking to revise Marx, Andre Gorz had argued that changes in the nature of production had bid 'farewell to the working class' and led to the creation of a majority, post-industrial 'non-class' (Gorz, 1982). With 'no job security, or no class identity' (p 69), having been 'expelled from production' (p 69), the non-class no longer had any clear occupational identity. Its members moved from 'one job to another', doing 'any old thing' which 'anyone could do' (p 71). Much of what Gorz wrote about then, when the 'second machine age' was still in its infancy, may have been premature, but it is an apt description of the working lives of many people now, and also the way they feel about them. (See Silva, 2015, for a vivid contemporary account in the US.)

Guy Standing (2011) revives Gorz to announce that, rather than 'a reserve army', neoliberal capitalism has created a global 'precariat' that has been cut adrift from the established working class, and has little contact with and little faith in its trade union and other 'labour movement' organisations. For Standing, the precariat is not only growing but, because of the uncertainty of modern labour markets, 'almost any of us' could fall into it. It is also 'far from being homogeneous' (p 13), stretching from students surviving on a series of temporary jobs, through illegal immigrants, to pensioners taking on casual work in order to pay medical bills. It is also geographically dispersed across developed and developing nations alike, with its heartland in China, 'the engine of the global precariat' (p 107).

Unlike Gorz's 'non-class' which, because of its increased marginality is no longer capable of becoming a self-conscious class 'for itself' in the way that Marx prophesied for the proletariat, according to Standing, the precariat's experience of 'anger, anomie, anxiety and alienation' has made it the 'new dangerous class' that his title borrows from Marx. Because it does not feel part of the solidaristic labour movement, the precariat increasingly takes direct action outside of it – and invariably it is young people who lead these often spontaneous initiatives. Despite Standing's optimism, such youthful unity of action is difficult to imagine, as disparities between the 2011 student protests and urban riots revealed (Allen and Ainley, 2012). If the traditional working class, or rather traditional class politics, is now disappearing in the way that Gorz predicted, Standing is largely dismissive of any relationship that what remains of the traditional labour movement can make with the precariat. But this should not mean that trade unions and other organisations abandon efforts to develop new types of strategies for the 'disorganised' working class of the 21st century.

Yet whatever the merits of Standing and Gorz's arguments, there can be no doubt about the growth of a 'new poor'. In 2015, the

Joseph Rowntree Foundation (Davis et al, 2015) found 40% of British families in 'relative poverty', that is, too poor to participate fully in society, with the number of those on less than what was referred to as the 'minimum income level' (put at just over £16,000 for a single person) up by a third from 5.9 million in 2008/09 to 8.1 million. The Foundation reported that for most working households, the increase in numbers below the minimum income level can be explained 'more by stagnant wages and cuts to in-work benefits than people having less work' (see also Clark and Heath, 2014; Lansley and Mack, 2015). These were Gordon Brown's working tax credits that the Conservatives sought to cut, claiming that, instead of the state subsidising low-paying employers, wages would rise to the new national minimum in the 'high wage, low tax, low welfare' working people's paradise Cameron promised his 2015 Party conference.

In relation specifically to schooling, based on Office for Budgetary Responsibility (OBR) figures, the Fabian Society forecast 3.69 million children living in poverty by 2030, up from nearly 1.5 million at the time of the study in 2015 (reported in *The Independent*, 24 June 2015). Media reaction, like similar warnings from Church of England bishops, was typically cast in terms of 'two nations', although again, in class terms, these are a different 'two nations' from Disraeli's Victorian originals, but reflected more another Victorian division between the 'respectable' and 'rough' working class, or the 'deserving' and 'undeserving poor'.

By the end of 2015, unemployment, at least in terms of how it is officially measured, had fallen to 1.75 million from well over 2.5 million at the peak of the recession. However, the labour market may be approaching full capacity with a figure of 5.5%, or 1 in 17, of the economically active population – around three times the postwar level – now constituting an acceptable level of unemployment or new definition of 'full employment'. With cuts to benefits, the new RAL finds itself typically not living off social security but churning in and out of insecure, low-paid, short-term, often part-time jobs. Add to this jobseekers forced into 'self-employment' to set up businesses without any real turnover, together with those on zero-hours contracts who spend more time not working. A more realistic calculation of under- if not unemployment might then provide a figure of around 10%. At the time of writing, for 18- to 24-year-olds not in full-time education or training, levels of unemployment may even be rising (EHRC, 2015). This is an ominous development because, as noted, young people are among those finding it most difficult to join the labour market, but also the first to be likely to leave it.

They find themselves forced into temporary, low-paid, subsidised work presented as 'training' or 'apprenticeships', or forced to take on student debt in the hope of eventual secure and at least semi-professional occupations. Meanwhile, they run up a down-escalator of devaluing qualifications in lengthening periods in school, college and university. This is because the implication of an emerging 'pear-shaped' occupational structure, as opposed to an hourglass – let alone a diamond-shaped one – is that instead of a limited amount of upward social mobility, as in the postwar past, most people are nowadays more at risk of downward social mobility.

## Summary

This chapter has described how long-term social trends have altered the class structure of English society. The division of knowledge and labour embodied in the postwar social pyramid has been eroded between the non-manual, middle class and the manual working class. The pyramid has gone pear-shaped under the pressure of general downward social mobility forming a new middle working/working middle class. Beneath them a section of the unskilled and unrespectable traditional working class has expanded into a new rough, so-called 'underclass', or RAL, in permanent precarity. The result is that many of the current generation of young people are likely to be the first to occupy a lower occupational/class position than their parents, in spite of being much better qualified. They have been bamboozled by too 'great expectations' of their extended and intensified educational efforts, which paradoxically leave them less well equipped than previous generations to deal with deteriorating employment prospects in a deregulated labour market.

As the next chapter will emphasise, this contradiction has generated mounting hysteria and competitive desperation around education for those running up the down-escalator of depreciating qualifications. This has serious implications for the continued legitimacy of education, and has resulted in attempts to change the direction of policy to create a 'new correspondence' between education and the labour market, this time at tertiary rather than secondary level.

# FOUR

# RUNNING UP A DOWN-ESCALATOR

Chapter One recalled how education in the 1950s and 1960s enabled a minority of individuals to 'move up' the old social class pyramid. It enabled them to cross the great divide in knowledge and labour that used to exist in the employed population between manual and non-manual work. This possibility was related to increased opportunities for entering expanding white-collar, managerial and professional employment. These career opportunities encouraged moves towards comprehensive schools and away from selection at 11+ since more than a limited 'pool of ability' came to be regarded as 'educable'. They were recommended by the Robbins Report (1963) to progress to higher education.

It is important to retain this history because, contrary to Conservative mythology, comprehensive schools did not bring this period of limited absolute upward social mobility to an end. Therefore returning to selective grammar schooling will not restore it. Rather, for a time, comprehensive schooling ensured supply continued to meet demand – at least until the demand dried up. This is clearly seen by comparing the US during the same period, where all-through comprehensive high schools had existed since the Second World War, but where similarly limited absolute upward social mobility also ended in the late 1970s (Aronowitz, 2008). High school graduates, but also more and more university graduates, were then left 'all dressed up with nowhere to go'.

In this chapter it is argued that, with the increasingly restricted opportunities for young people summarised in Chapters Two and Three, education has once again become primarily an agent of social control that nowadays substitutes for wage discipline in the absence of work. Or rather, substitutes for the youth wage with hopes of an adult one. Extended education and training can then be seen to have played a large part, alongside housing, policing and regional policy, in shaping and reinforcing the new class divisions of knowledge and labour outlined in Chapter Three, as well as in seeking a new correspondence of education with remaining employment.

## The new student experience

Despite all the claims made for it as a doctrine of individual salvation, education at all levels teaches people to know their place, and only in exceptional cases enables them to leave it. The exception is then made the rule, at least in popular misrepresentation. In hopes of achieving such a distant goal, from childhood on into 'prolonged youth' (Bynner, 2005), up to the new age of majority at 25 marked by payment of the full National Living Wage, pupil-students face a series of hurdles that mark critical divergences onto one pathway or another. Without necessarily realising it, individuals can get locked into one of these tracks. Recovery from what later becomes evident is relegation to an inferior route (defined both by subject and institution), while not impossible, then becomes increasingly difficult.

These crunch points – and the pressure put on young people by family, peers and themselves – intensify in frequency throughout their educational careers: once every four years after initial testing in primary, but then again on entry to secondary school, after retesting that the government is imposing but teachers are resisting. Guided 'option choices' are then made after three years followed by two years to the first critical cut-off point of five A–C GCSEs. Whether on the academic or vocational route from then on, modularised assessment avoids the trauma of end-of-course, 'sudden-death' examinations that the government wants to revert to. On the other hand, it breaks the individual's scores down into a running total (like the US Grade Point Averages, GPAs) that there is incessant pressure to maintain. If these add up to three 'good' A-levels, options are open for application to the hierarchy of higher education (HE).

Yet such is the current competition between universities for students, recovery is again possible even at this late stage, since all degrees are officially equal. As long as you pass the first year, of course – if only with a 'fuck-it 40' pass mark, as Cheeseman's undergraduate interviewees put it (2011, and see also Ainley, 2008). Then you can leave the high point of the student experience which is 'freshers' behind, and return to 'the student bubble' for two more years of semester/module tests that you desperately hope add up to more than 'a deadly Desmond' (a 2:2 grade). Otherwise, you have lost your fee/loan investment and might as well have left at the age of 18 for what employment you could find – with or without 'apprenticeship'. For those who persist, pressure, stress and cramming intensify until graduation, removing any pleasure in learning. Compensatory 'pleasures of being a student' can then assume the aspect of tedious obligation (see Cheeseman, 2011).

There is more risk of failure for those who can least afford to take it. A lack of confidence in their ability 'to hack it' afflicts students from poorer and minority parental backgrounds, and limits their aspirations. They often choose to 'play safe' at seemingly less demanding and local new universities with people like themselves. This is a powerful attractor up and down 'the endless chain of hierarchy and condescension that passes for a system [of higher education] in England' (Scott, 2015), and one which, moreover, is raddled with snobbery, sexism and racism. Students accept all this and their mounting debts with a resigned fatalism. For example, this comment from a survey on fees at a new university: "The problem as I see it is that most young people know they are being 'ripped off' but there is nothing we can really do about it."

The odds on gaining a 2:1 or first-class honours are good, however, since these are now achieved by about 70% of graduates as compared with about 20% of a much smaller cohort pre-expansion. They enable entry to usually only a one-year Master's (when 'real HE' begins for two years in the US), if not endless internships (Perlin, 2011). Even on this academic 'Royal Road', capped by a PhD (increasingly required to teach in HE), "It doesn't matter how far you go in the English education system, they'll fail you in the end!", as former London schools Tsar Tim Brighouse quips. This is the real 'student journey' that is so much celebrated and regulated at universities – and it is an increasingly long one! It is not so much an 'experience' as a process. So it is no wonder that references to schools as 'exam factories' proliferate (as in Hutchins for the NUT, 2015), or that during the 2011 'student spring' the students in the Really Open University referred on their posters to their own University of Leeds as a 'sausage factory'.

Nearly all young people today are subject to what Phil Cohen, in *Rethinking the youth question* (1997, p 284 et seq), called the 'career code'. This had previously only been followed by a minority of grammar school-educated traditionally middle-class young people making an institutionalised transition from school to work, and from living at home to living away by way of term-time residential HE on campus. This 'career code' has now been extended to and largely accepted by 'striving' parents and children who think of themselves as belonging to the new working middle/middle working class. Only a minority of 14+-year-olds are diverted to the once majority second-best 'vocation code' of 'apprenticeship'. As Cohen warned, 'this is not just the material effect of youth unemployment on school transitions; it is about changes in the codes of cultural reproduction' (1997, p 233). It is another reason vocational options are not so easily revived, especially in the absence of the employment to which they once led.

The 'career code' does, however, impose a coherent structure on young people's lives to make them comprehensible to their parents and themselves. Education becomes their occupation but, like most jobs or occupations, it is subsidiary to individuals' more immediate social concerns. It is merely a tedium to be 'gone through' to get somewhere else. This is what Lave and McDermott (2002) call 'estranged learning'. Without any real shared practical activity to which acquired knowledge and skills can be applied, learners' behaviour is assessed instead. Appropriate behaviour is honed in the endless 'presentations' students are expected to undertake throughout school, college and on into university, and in the relentless presentation of self that is necessary for interviews and in CVs, as well as on Facebook [sic]. Insofar as these performances of 'interpersonal' and 'soft skills' have any retail value, it is in self-regulated and stereotypically feminine customer care.

For education at all levels, this creates a situation where learning (increasingly reduced to training) becomes an end in itself – and a dead end at that! The result is profoundly alienating for teachers and students alike, as institutionalised education turns into its opposite. It forecloses possibilities of learning in pursuit of the next examination hoop to jump through, certifying only ability to pass on to the next stage. There is thus decreasing intrinsic interest or content in this institutionalised 'learning' – let alone any enlightenment! The end result is students and their teachers forced by managers and inspectors to conform to a tyranny of transparency that spells out in every detail what will be required for quantified assessment. 'Students', as one of them wrote in a final year education studies project at the University of Greenwich more than 10 years ago,

> ... learn to connect their self-esteem and what they may achieve in life to their exam results.... Over-assessment has made subject knowledge and understanding a thing of the past as students are put through a routine year after year, practising what exactly to write and where in preparation for exams.

In an historical and sociological context, such 'scholastic careers' can be said to have substituted for real ones in employment. In place of the wage as the main means of social control (over young men especially), education has become key to social control over young people. It always was, just as the need to 'shackle minds' and 'civilise the class as a whole' to 'educate our masters' was a fundamental reason for the reluctant acceptance of mass schooling by England's Victorian ruling class (Johnson, 1976). Subsequently, 1960s sociology explained 'juvenile delinquency' by a minority of working-class boys (the peak age for which offences always anticipated the school leaving age by one year) as due to failure by that minority to 'settle down' with 'a steady job' and 'a girlfriend'. Thus the schools 'gentled the masses', only today much more so.

At the same time, and as noted in Chapter One, it is important to reaffirm the worth of past reforms to education – from progressive primary schools through comprehensive secondary schools with inclusion of special needs on to widened participation in further, higher and adult education. These allowed room for innovations and challenges that sustained the momentum of reform even after the economic conditions that enabled it had dissipated. A return to an education system that serves to keep a lid on aspiration while still officially encouraging it would require a prolonged structural readjustment. It could be argued that this began with Labour Prime Minister James Callaghan's Ruskin College speech in 1976 in which he announced the end of his Party's comprehensive experiment.

## 'Independent state schools'

As a matter of overt policy, however, such a reversal was not attempted until the coalition under the direction of neo-conservative Education Secretary Michael Gove and neoliberal Universities' Minister David Willetts. Despite their reported mutual antipathy, they shared a belief that too many children were succeeding in state education. Or rather, that too many of the wrong sort of children had gone to the wrong sort of universities. This needed to be reversed by, on the one hand, making the qualifying exams harder to pass and, on the other, making HE more expensive by tripling fees.

They were only partly successful in realising these aims, and neither Willetts nor Gove lasted the full term of the coalition, at least not as education ministers. Nevertheless, their immediate successors were primed to continue with these policies along the same road, in particular Nicky Morgan at Education, with her endorsement not only of more free schools and academies but also more university technical colleges (UTCs)/STEM (science, technology, engineering and maths) schools and also studio schools closely related to specific employers.

The latter peddle a limited curriculum supposedly related to the needs of local employment, like the one in Lutterworth, Leicestershire that claims links to nearby engineering and logistics firms, as well as more generally to retail, hospitality and leisure services.

'Free schools', set up by groups of parents, charities and others, encouraged by the DfE, have been widely criticised for haphazard duplication of existing provision. This criticism misses the point: the surplus places free schools provide offer parental choice in a local market, never mind that there are shortages elsewhere. Modelled on and in some cases sponsored by Swedish private *friskolor*, free schools are allowed partial selection of pupils by 'aptitude'. This results in less children on free school meals, with special needs, and with English as a second language compared with local authority schools. Despite this and various scandals and irregularities resulting in the closure of several of them, free schools continue to expand.

It is not for nothing that so many educational consultancies, edu-businesses, hedge fund managers and Tory grandees have supported these nominally charitable independent but state-funded free schools and academies. Even if not run for the profits promised by Gove but so far ruled out by Morgan, related business interests can be expanded in linked activities, such as supplying and then selling on IT systems. Others, like the late and unlamented former HM Inspector Chris Woodhead's Cognita Group, as well as the Dubai-based GEM Group, with another former HM Inspector, Mike Tomlinson, on its board, have been waiting in the wings for some time to start up cut-price crammers. (And see Ball, 2015, on Pearson's 'the world's largest edu-business'.)

Take as an example the Oasis chain: a nominally Christian foundation started from small beginnings by a social entrepreneur/philanthropist, it has taken over care and social services provision as well as primary and secondary schools from local authorities, with links also to its own housing association. Like others, the chain provides its own teacher training and in-house staff development programmes. Little – or not so little – empires are thus accreted, with the chief executive of the Harris

Federation of schools earning more than £375,000 a year and some 'super heads', who manage several schools at once, over £250,000.

The Church of England remains the largest of such groupings, continuing the provision it, Catholic and Jewish schools were allowed under the Education Act 1944. This was subsequently extended to 'faith schools', favoured by New Labour despite the dire precedent of sectarian schooling in Northern Ireland. Some of these schools teach 'creation science' in parallel with National Curriculum biology, while others ignore recommended approaches to sex and relationship education (see BHA, 2015), not to mention the financial and other abuses that have come to light under other 'approved sponsors'.

The justification for a former carpet salesman, Lord Harris, presiding over such a large part of public education as is provided by his Harris Academy chain, is that such 'entrepreneurs' contribute to what its advocates call 'a self-improving system', constantly 'raising standards' through competition. In the familiar formula of the new market state, the schools are semi-privatised but state-subsidised so they are free from 'bureaucratic' local authority control. Instead, in a national system nationally and no longer locally administered, schools are contracted out from the centre, or, as this becomes increasingly remote and bureaucratic, delegated to the oversight of an additional layer of appointed regional commissioners. These independent state schools are not required to follow the National Curriculum, and they enjoy other 'freedoms', such as not having to employ trained teachers. They are also completely removed from any local democratic accountability, and under the proposed Education and Adoption Bill will lose even locally appointed school governors.

The stage has thus been set for further expansion to a fully-fledged free market. However, the legal obligation to provide free state provision from ages 5 to now 18 remains. The only way around this would be for 'council schools' to supply basic provision guaranteed by a voucher. Other schools could then charge parents to top up these vouchers at more or less expensive 'independent' provision. This would be along the lines of the US charter schools described by Diane

Ravitch as playing such a large part in what she called 'the death and life of the great American school system' (2010).

Half of all state secondary schools and 4,835 out of all 21,500 state-funded schools in England had 'converted' to academies, as well as about 300 set up from scratch as free schools (including the UTCs referred to above), by the time of Parliament's dissolution in 2015. The acceleration of what had been a more gradual process under New Labour was picking up and, as Jenny Turner wrote in the *London Review of Books* (2015), 'Barely under control'. Cameron has since announced his government's intention to academise or 'free' all state schools.

Full marketisation would still be very hazardous, however, especially with a 'big bang' voucherised approach, despite the example of university fees that can be regarded as paperless vouchers. Vouchers would also paradoxically bring the private schools into the state system, as potentially parents could also discount their vouchers against fees there. However, this would mean the state subsidising the private sector at a cost that even Sir Keith Joseph, Mrs Thatcher's *éminence grise*, Education Minister and convinced voucherite, realised would be prohibitive (see Denham and Garnett, 2002, p 432).

Indications are therefore that state schools will continue along the lines mapped out under Gove, apart from some expansion of UTCs alongside other free schools and possible returns of 'technical' or 'vocational' equivalents to A-level linked to 'apprenticeships', although in October 2015, Morgan succumbed to pressure in her Party for further overt selection by allowing a grammar school in Tonbridge to open an 'annex' 10 miles away in Sevenoaks. If this passes judicial review, it may set a precedent for other surviving grammar schools to open similar offshoots, perhaps leading to chains of academically selective state-funded grammar schools as opponents fear. (Or the 1998 law against new grammars could be revoked.)

Schools, colleges and universities are not included in the regeneration promised to Northern 'powerhouse' cities in return for elected mayors with cabinets. Latham has described these as 'the optimal internal management arrangement for privatised local government services' (2011, pp 215). Instead, free schools and academies will be overseen by a new unelected bureaucracy of regional commissioners. The more organic regional regroupings of universities envisioned by Byrne's rebooting of Robbins (2014) will also not be supported, while FE colleges are being closed and merged under cover of BIS-sponsored area reviews.

Competition between universities is to be spurred by a Teaching Quality Framework operated by a new central Office for Students. Universities will be rewarded, not only for their teaching excellence, but also for widening participation, by being allowed to raise their fees in line with inflation – initially perhaps. New entrants to the 'HE' market will also be encouraged with students in private colleges already comprising 10% of state-funded undergraduates receiving roughly £700 million a year, and described by McGettigan (2015) as a 'subprime undergraduate sector'. Like some of the free schools and academies, some private colleges have been implicated in irregularities such as 'chugging for students' so as to claim funding for them – a repetition of the Independent Learning Accounts scam by private training agencies (NAO, 2002). From primary to postgraduate schools, this all reflects Conservative belief in 'competition driving up standards'.

## Opportunities to be unequal

Michael Gove seemed to share a similar delusion that there could be 'grammar school education for all' (as Harold Wilson had deviously described his government's new comprehensive schools). Yet, by definition, grammar schooling – like private schooling – is premised on the selection of a minority. Like Mrs Thatcher, Gove reversed Old Labour's comprehensive slogan of equal opportunities into opportunities to be unequal. If starting points were equalised by the same schooling for everyone (although the exemption from the National Curriculum for private and free schools was inconsistent with this), 'fair outcomes' could be achieved. So Gove promoted his policies as restoring standards and the credibility of public examinations. He accused the previous Labour government of making exams 'too easy' and giving what he considered to be inferior vocational qualifications the equivalent status to traditional academic qualifications in school league tables.

Gove justified his approach by borrowing from US educationalist E.D. Hirsch. Hirsch proposed that it is possible to identify 'core knowledge' in each subject discipline, and accused US schools of not teaching this but concentrating on 'skills', resulting in a 'knowledge deficit' (Hirsch, 2006) – such 'powerful knowledge' should be learned by everyone so that they can compete on equal terms in examinations of it. This is very different from classical notions of powerful knowledge, such as Aristotle's 'knowledge necessary to rule'. This was not an accumulation of information for regurgitation in exams, but knowledge of the rules by which existing information could be ordered and new knowledge created. The implication of the Hirsch approach was that education is about the uncritical transfer down the generations of 'the best which has been thought and said,' as Gove parroted Matthew Arnold's 1867 definition of culture, hence 'a study of perfection' (1939, p 143).

This enthusiasm for extremely narrow, unchanging and traditional notions of 'culture' was far from 'modernising' and promoting social justice by contributing to upward social mobility and stimulating economic growth – somehow! In fact, Gove aimed to restrict success in end-of-course, summary examinations to smaller numbers of candidates. This was the way to 'win the education race with our international competitors'. So Gove's 2010 White Paper, *The importance of teaching* (DfE, 2010), outlined plans to reform teaching, following 'high-performing countries such as Finland, Singapore, Hong Kong and New Zealand' (para 2.3). Teachers were dispatched to Shanghai to watch maths lessons in 'high-performing' schools to see how this could be done. Setting the agenda for the new Conservative government, Morgan followed in Gove's footsteps, promising a more traditional primary schooling where children would sit in rows chanting the 12 times table (!) and concentrate on rote learning punctuation and grammar, while she proposed replacing football by rugby for 'character building' in secondary schools.

There are harrowing tales of the pressures inflicted on young people in South Korea and Japan, where children serve double shifts after school with either private tutors or in cramming schools. Most English children, regardless of their performance level, would not tolerate this sort of environment, and nor would their parents. Still, computer clubs on street corners and even in supermarkets encourage them to spend their evenings and weekends working through tedious on-screen teaching programmes, often supported by private tutoring of variable quality.

## Redrawing the academic and vocational divide

Brushing aside such considerations in his eagerness to make headlines, Gove – described by Ken Jones as (to his opponents) 'a politician of uniquely repellent qualities' (2016, p 194) – announced the introduction of completely new examinations, English Baccalaureate Certificates (EBCs). These were to replace GCSEs in English, maths, history, geography and science, which would be harder to pass. This would create two tiers of subjects, reminiscent of the pre-1986 GCE-CSE divide. It would also lead to schools prioritising these exams and marginalising others. Gove was defeated over the EBCs following a well-organised and broad campaign that included prominent individuals in the Arts, fearing for the future of non-EBC subjects such as music and drama. So instead, Gove announced new GCSEs that replaced coursework with written end-of-course exams enabling more differentiation between students via a new nine-point grading system. Teaching the new courses has been phased in from September 2015. Repeated calls to phase out GCSEs in favour of a school leaving qualification at 18 are therefore likely to fall on deaf ears, unless secondary teachers take some action, like their primary colleagues' protests against entry-level tests.

GCE A-levels were treated in the same way as GCSEs, as Gove sought to restore their 'gold standard' status. Despite the A-level becoming a 'mass' qualification, with approaching 1 million entries and with one in four candidates gaining an A grade, new 'knowledge-based' A-level syllabuses are to be introduced from September 2016. The current system, with AS-level qualification certifying completion of the first year of the course, is to be scrapped, despite remaining popular with universities as it provides them with evidence of applicants' progress, apart from their teachers' recommendations for them!

If changes to the examinations were designed to put clearer water between success and failure and between the 'sheep' and the 'goats', then the division between academic and vocational learning was also to be redefined. As noted in Chapter One, vocational education courses emerged in schools alongside those in FE colleges from the early 1980s, and coincided with increases in staying on. This led to the growth of the 'new sixth' in schools, sixth form colleges and academic centres within FE colleges. They reflected the collapse of opportunities in the youth labour market and rejection of the MSC's 'training without jobs'. Following Lord Dearing's three successive reviews of the National Curriculum in the 1990s, 'vocational pathways' were introduced as alternatives to academic specialisation for 14+-year-olds.

Unlike some other European countries, where vocational education has a much closer relationship with workplace training and occupational progression, vocational education in English schools has been almost exclusively classroom-based and delivered by teachers. Designed to reflect the growth of the post-Fordist workplace and officially welcomed by employer representatives, there was little evidence individual employers understood, or paid much attention to, the new qualifications (Allen and Ainley, 2008b). Employers certainly didn't favour students who had followed the vocational route, but continued to prefer young people with GCSEs and A-levels – that is, if they recruited young people at all!

Instead, vocational qualifications such as BTECs and GNVQs came to be used as 'second chance' routes into HE. As a result, they continued to have low academic status, and to improve this, Labour's Curriculum 2000 redesigned them to be more like academic qualifications (Allen, 2007). However, this alienated the very students they were established to cater for. Given equivalent status to academic qualifications in league tables, and in some cases counting for two or more GCSEs, many schools entered entire cohorts of their students, thus improving their league table point scores. On coming to office, Michael Gove commissioned Professor Alison Wolf to review vocational provision in schools, signalling his intent to remove vocational qualifications from league tables unless they met strict criteria. In future, vocational qualifications would also only count as equivalent to one GCSE. Gove's reforms were therefore a response to what was considered to be the 'credential inflation' of the previous decades.

Widening entitlement to Hirsch's 'core knowledge' through locking all secondary schools into a grammar school National Curriculum also privileged academic over vocational learning. This approach did not find favour with all Tories, especially Kenneth (now Lord) Baker, successor to Keith Joseph as Mrs Thatcher's Education Secretary and creator of the National Curriculum. He now favours an academic vocational/grammar technical divide at 14+ (Baker, 2013), and so has ploughed on with UTCs. These are free schools sponsored by universities or companies with vocational specialisms linked to their courses or businesses, although students continue with GCSEs in mandatory subjects. Education was thus divided into two main 'pathways', as Baker's collaborator Lord Dearing called them in 1996.

In the absence of labour market progression and distinct occupational routes, this provides a means to separate learners remaining in full-time education. Before the 2015 general election, Labour also committed itself to such a 'two nation' approach, announcing it would introduce a technical baccalaureate to be delivered in rebranded FE colleges and leading to two-year reinvented foundation degrees. In his subsequent and successful leadership bid, Jeremy Corbyn proposed a rebranded National Education Service to include 'colleges working in partnership with employers to mutually accredit apprenticeships and courses that offer high quality transferable skills', with 'councils and government agencies' using 'public procurement contracts to guarantee good apprenticeships', thus joining the new consensus.

## Selection and differentiation

Alongside the increased pressure on examinations to differentiate students, there has also been a proliferation of the different types of schools described above. The re-announcement of 'grammar schooling for all' – if not of grammar schools themselves, beyond those persisting, as noted in Chapter One, in nearly 1 in 10 LEAs and their annexes above – has thus not led to the rigid tripartite differentiation of the 1944 Act. Then, as well as over 1,200 LEA-run grammar schools, until 1974 there were up to 200 direct grant schools providing 25% of places free of charge to children who had spent at least two years in maintained primary schools, with a further 25% of places allowed to be paid for by the LEA. Moreover, selective examination for entry to grammar schooling is no longer made to appear natural today, as it was after the Second World War by supposedly scientific IQ testing.

During the early years of New Labour government, the emphasis had also been on 'standards, not structures'. Rather than differentiation between schools, differentiation within schools would reassure 'aspiring parents' that their children could still do well in state schools. Accordingly, 'personalised' approaches differentiated 'gifted and talented' pupils from the not gifted and not talented. Sorting by different 'learning styles' reached down even into infant schools, where teachers were encouraged to group together HAPs, MAPs and LAPs (higher, middle and lower achieving pupils). These were 'the gifted and talented, the just plain average and the struggling', as a 2005 White Paper unsubtly distinguished them (DfES, 2005, p 20).

After winning the 2001 election, however, New Labour had introduced the slogan of 'choice and diversity', sounding alarm bells for some of its supporters. Central to this was the establishment of 'specialist' status, where schools were allowed to promote a particular area of the curriculum. New Labour also introduced 'academies', giving control of 200 'under-performing' schools to private sponsors. It was under the coalition, however, that differentiation of schools became a key policy, with many more schools bribed, forced or otherwise cajoled into becoming academies, while new free schools continue to be encouraged.

Debate continues over whether becoming an academy in itself leads to better performance. (See the continuing critique of official data by the Anti-Academies Alliance – http://antiacademies.org.uk/) At the least, allowing schools to convert to academy status has enabled existing high-performing state schools with more prosperous intakes to maintain their advantages. Others that were converted after not performing so well, initially at least, sometimes improved from a low base. Additionally, there have been repeated allegations of academies covertly selecting more able and well-to-do students.

In relation to private schools, the latest Independent Schools Council annual census reported a slight rise to 517,113 pupils to January 2015 – up 1% from the year before. This was mainly attributed to the partial economic recovery, but also to proportions of international students rising to 5.3% (from 4.4% 30 years ago). According to Andrew Halls, Head of King's College School, Wimbledon, quoted in *The Guardian* (5 December 2014), schools like his are becoming 'finishing schools for the children of oligarchs'. Parents who are being squeezed out by the 40% rise in fees since 2007 to an average of £30,369 a year boarding and £13,194 for a day school place (£15,500 in London), fall back on paying a 'school premium' for homes in desirable state school catchment areas. Many more parents resort to private tutoring.

As a result, the concept of the 'neighbourhood comprehensive', so close to the heart of many education campaigners, has been given a new meaning. The original ideal of a good local school for all children perhaps survives best in local authority primary schools, despite denominational primaries accentuating residential differentiation. The parental hysteria and child stress that annually accompanies the secondary school applications process when, this year, one in seven nationally did not get their first choice (almost one in three in London) was reflected in the 20,235 appeals against secondary admissions in 2015 (*The Times*, 28 February 2015). Demographic pressures are also adding to overall shortages of school places.

## Aiming higher?

The last two decades have seen huge increases in attendance at HE so that it has moved swiftly from a minority to a mass system. As is the case with education in general, and as also noted in Chapter One, these increased participation rates are closely related to changes in labour market opportunities – or, rather, the lack of them. As Chapters Two and Three made clear, 'a good degree' is now essential for hopes of most secure employment. The Blair-Brown governments set the ambitious target of half of 18- to 30-year-olds being in HE by 2010. Although this was never achieved, by the time Labour left office, a third of 18+ women and a quarter of men were applying for degree courses, despite the introduction of £1,000 fees in 1997, which were subsequently tripled and then tripled again. Fees were backed by student loans, with repayments linked to future earnings, so that students who could not afford to pay them off would leave university with huge debts.

Expanding university education had been central to Labour's 'upskilling for globalisation' strategy, for example, in the 2006 Leitch *Review of skills: Prosperity for all in a global economy*. But the coalition Universities' Minister, David Willetts, was under pressure to reduce student numbers. He also wanted to further differentiate institutions from one another by allowing them to charge what the market would bear, although this did not happen. Anxious not to be seen as offering an 'inferior product', almost all HE institutions announced that they would charge the maximum fee. This was capped at £9,000 by a compromise with the Liberal Democrats in the coalition. Universities needed the money since they were now dependent on student fees to fund their courses – apart from for the still centrally funded STEM subjects, as well as a few 'strategic and vulnerable' subjects.

Despite fee rises, young people have continued to enter HE in large numbers in hopes of secure and at least semi-professional careers. In 2014, for the first time, more than half a million students took up an offer of a place at a UK university. Most were English home students, with women now making up 60% of the undergraduate population (although this proportion would be reduced if courses in education and health were excluded). On some prestigious programmes, such as medicine and law, however, the proportion of women is 70%, although a much smaller proportion of consultants or judges are women. This points towards the 'feminisation' of HE that has been blamed for putting some boys off applying and for the reactive 'lad culture' among some of those remaining. Certainly, girls are on average better qualified to apply and possibly more motivated to do so, especially as there are less immediate other opportunities for them, such as seem to account for 'the lost boys' who leave school from 14+ on and who do not show up in FE or on apprenticeships, there no longer being any way to track them now that the Careers Service has been privatised and disbanded.

In 2015, notwithstanding some pick up in the economy, relentless propaganda for 'apprenticeships' and a demographic fall in numbers of 18- to 19-year-olds, the desperate competition between nearly all universities for fee-paying students made it easier than ever to get in, and so more applied in the absence of other alternatives. (And also because this was the last year maintenance grants would be available.) With this increased participation, and because elite universities have not – at least for the time being – been able to distinguish themselves through fee increases, institutions seek to differentiate themselves in other ways. Universities have been gradually released from rationing the most qualified applicants among themselves. Consequently, all but two of them (ie. Oxford and Cambridge), as well as the London School of Economics, are in a frantic competition to cram in as many as possible since their funding depends on it! In other words, to poach students from one another, creaming off students who thought they were heading for more 'middling' universities but who can now use the post-results 'clearing' to trade up, 'trade down' from the universities' point of view!

Even with this free-for-all, widening participation has not led to a more equitable HE system. As Danny Dorling pointed out in the *Times Higher Education* (12 February 2015), the coalition's boast to have increased participation from the poorest postcodes has to be set against the still larger rise from the most affluent ones. As he indicated, 'It is mathematically possible for poorer groups to have by far the largest increase in entry rates while the absolute differences still widen.' This is what has happened:

> Rounding to whole numbers, for every three children from the poorest areas going to the "poshest" (high-entry tariff) universities in 2014, some 21 children from the most advantaged areas also went. Three years earlier, in 2011, the respective figures were two and 19. To put this another way, for every extra child from a poorer area allowed in to a high-tariff university in 2014, an extra two from the best-off areas arrived within the same year (*Times Higher Education*, 2015, p 81).

Or, as Peter Scott (2013, p 50) summarised it: 'The focus has shifted from encouraging lower-cost provision to privileging highly qualified students, whose choice, therefore, is now being enhanced at the expense of their less qualified peers.'

Teacher-student ratios vary from 1:26.3 at the University of East London to 1:10.2 at University College London, while Oxford and Cambridge maintain a tutorial system of individual undergraduate teaching. These latter have financial and real estate holdings worth £3 and £4 billion respectively – the next richest, Edinburgh, has £150 million. These resources are manifested in gross inequities in provision – a single Oxbridge college library often being bigger than many university libraries, for instance. The close links of elite universities with private schools have been remarked on so that students from these schools make up 39% of Cambridge undergraduates and 43.2% at Oxford at the last count. State school admissions to Cambridge dropped by nearly two percentage points in 2014, despite summer schools, masterclasses and open days to encourage them. Taking all universities together, graduates who attended private secondary schools were seven percentage points more likely than graduates from state schools to go on to professional employment (Sutton Trust, Press Release, 18 December 2014).

The system is self-reinforcing, and consequently, the general rule is 'the older the university, the younger, whiter, more male and posher are its students' (Ainley, 2015) – although Warwick and Bath are exceptions that prove the rule. (Strangely, elite universities – notably the top two – somehow manage to balance their overall gender intakes. They say this is due to their preponderance in science and technology, but in practice it must be harder for girls to get into them.) Oxbridge – within which again there is an elaborate, jockeying hierarchy of colleges – is thus the apex of the giant sorting machine that is English education. Meanwhile, those from lower socioeconomic groups are relegated to the lower reaches of the student population. They obtain lower-end 'graduate jobs' if they are lucky. The opposite happens with Oxbridge graduates, earning on average £7,600 more per annum on starting employment compared with those from the new (post-1992) universities (Sutton Trust, Press Release, 18 December 2014). According to the graduate recruitment agency High Fliers, in 2014, 40% of top graduate recruiters target just 15 universities, with one in seven targeting just ten. Institutions targeted by employers are those at the top of university rankings that are based on teaching quality and academic research as well as student destinations.

As McCullough (2015) comments, 'It is not necessarily the case that all of those universities not in the Russell Group offer to their students an inferior quality of educational experience.' (Although it can be added that this tends to be the case, as reflected in the staff-student ratios and resources above. However, there have also been complaints about, for example, Russell Group University of Bristol in 2013 that, as a result of 'cramming them in', teaching for some undergraduates reduced to a few hours per week.) Rather, as McCullough continues, 'the status of the increasing numbers of qualifications awarded is not regarded as particularly valuable in the job markets.'

Students and parents are well aware of the social hierarchy of subjects and institutions. Many can see that, as Michael Bailey and Des Freedman predicted in 2011,

The UK's higher education system is to be transformed into a patchwork of academic supermarkets with, at one end, research-led Russell Group universities continuing to super-serve wealthier customers with a wide range of niche offerings while, at the other end, former polytechnics ... will be forced to clear their shelves of distinctive or idiosyncratic goods and to focus on those products for which there is already a clearly defined (mass) market. All shoppers, meanwhile, will have to pay higher prices. (p 2)

Or, as Alison Wolf puts it, universities are 'colonising areas of vocational education and training which were traditionally the preserve of ... vocational schools or colleges' (2015, p 74), with the consequence that 'more academically low achieving students are being recruited' (Wolf, 2015, p 67). With the dissolution of the colleges, FE students are being decanted into the unitary FE and HE sector that Palfreyman and Tapper call 'tertiary education (TE)' (2014, p v).

'The result,' as Naidoo and Jamieson suggested in 2005, may be a new correspondence with the labour market of 'a higher education system that produces a small elite of "self programmeable" workers who have learnt how to learn and are occupationally mobile, along with a large mass of "generic workers" who are exchangeable and disposable', that is, fungible. Certainly, in the social sciences and humanities, what you know is less important to employers than how you speak and write (spell). At the top of the university tree this results in the much complained-about dominance of a privately schooled elite over nearly all areas of public life. In the STEM subjects, at one end state support underwrites academic industrial/medical complexes sponsored by Big Pharma and the corporations. At the other, UTCs as well as various other links with schools, FE and training, widen participation to technician-level undergraduate STEM courses.

Yet because university application rates held up and fees did not put off applicants to reduce numbers, particularly those from 'disadvantaged' backgrounds, Willetts lost his 'great university gamble' (McGettigan, 2013) when he admitted that he did not expect to recover more than a third of what will add up to £330 billion of unpaid loans by 2046. His problem was intensified by the repayment threshold remaining at £21,000. This indicates the policy-makers behind the scheme under-estimated – or were even unaware of – the depreciation in graduate salaries together with the decline in 'graduate jobs' described in Chapters Two and Three.

It was likely the Conservative government would raise fees or alter the terms of repayment, or both. They have already frozen the £21,000 repayment threshold against inflation for undergraduate fees while turning means-tested maintenance grants into loans, thus removing the last remnant of public support for HE. This adds to the debts faced by the poorest students (up to £53,000 for a three-year degree course, according to the National Union of Students [NUS]) and so to the complex insurance/mortgage packages backing variously priced courses with different anticipated rates of return in employment that are the subject of speculative financial calculations by DBIS officials. Buyers still have to be found for these 'deals' who will want to avoid accusations of 'miss-selling' in future payment protection insurance (PPI)-type scenarios, such as have afflicted US SLABS (student loan asset-based securities).

If fees were uncapped completely, Oxford, Cambridge and a handful of other 'top' universities would charge as much as they could, pricing themselves out of the system, although reluctant to forsake all state subsidy. This would leave universities that could not compete on price to go to the wall. Many would collapse into virtual learning centres in the way that franchised courses to overseas partners and campuses abroad already sustain home provision for many universities and faculties within them. Other 'efficiencies' could further unravel institutions: for instance, through sharing back office support for merged services (as at Nottingham and Birmingham, Queen Mary and Warwick), if not through outright 'mergers' or takeovers, as of the London Institute of Education by University College London (UCL). Massive open online courses (MOOCs), available to anyone free of charge save for their certification, are also a threat to institutional control over their academic product.

Management buy-outs or corporate buy-ins are also possible, as well as continuing closures of under-recruiting/researching departments and other cost-cutting measures, such as the attack on pensions in the older universities. In the newer ones there may be more two-year 'degrees' taught over four terms a year. As seen, private 'universities' and colleges offering more cut-price deals to state-funded students will be further encouraged despite repeated scandals over their often dubious standards. A free market would then have fragmented what is left of a more or less coherent HE system. However, as with schools' vouchers, it is unlikely that the Tories will proceed directly to such a 'big bang' solution, as the consequences would be dramatic and incalculable. Indeed, Peter Scott warned of the possibility of 'a perfect storm' as a result of 'mounting turbulence' (2013, p 54).

## Student or 'apprentice'?

The university funding crisis has intensified the need to promote an alternative in the form of reinvented 'apprenticeships'. Before the 2015 general election, David Cameron promised 'Three million more apprenticeships – that means three million more engineers, accountants and project managers' (Cameron, 2015). This magical claim was matched by Ed Miliband who promised his 2014 Party Conference that the number of apprenticeships would match the number of university places. Then, after the election, the Conservative government unexpectedly announced the return of a levy on large employers to pay for apprenticeships. This provoked the Confederation of British Industry (CBI) into bitter recriminations since, as Martin Allen's ongoing research shows, most employers do not want or need apprenticeships, let alone to have to pay for them! And the few who do already pay for them themselves.

Martin's work also shows most apprenticeships continue to be low skilled and 'dead end'. Of the two million or so that have been created since 2010, the majority have been filled by adults, with many examples of existing staff being reclassified as 'apprentices' so that employers could access government subsidies. Two-thirds of apprenticeship starts are at level 2 – equivalent to a GCSE, a level to which most people are already qualified. They generally only last a year or less, and in most cases provide no employment guarantees and no opportunities to progress to a higher level. So they are not really apprenticeships at all, but 'another great training robbery' (Allen and Ainley, 2014), as officially confirmed over a year later by a damning report from Ofsted (2015).

By contrast, postwar apprenticeships were associated with manufacturing and provided a bridge between school and work for young male school leavers. Nowadays, the employment areas where apprenticeships are most easily available are in stereotypically female routine office work, health and social care, or retail, where they are linked to low-skilled jobs. There are a few very good schemes that lead to well-paid and skilled careers, but these exceptions are massively over-subscribed. BT and Rolls Royce apprenticeships, for example, attract more applicants per place than Oxford engineering degrees. Those with British Gas are in such high demand that suitable applicants have only about a 1 in 15 chance of being accepted. In comparison, qualified applicants for engineering at the University of Oxford have a 1 in 3 chance of success (Allen and Ainley, 2014, p 4).

There have been some changes with the new apprenticeships so that by 2014, at least two-thirds of starts were by people under 24, although only a quarter of these (120,000) were under 19. More young people also started advanced level schemes, even if numbers are still small (just 35,000 starts in 2013/14) compared to those enrolling on A-level or other courses in full-time education. But there are still only around 15,000 higher level apprenticeships currently operating, some of which include attending some form of HE, but only a very small number of these are started by school leavers. And also until now, the 'training' of apprentices has been carried out by private providers that then claim government funding. All training costs for those under 19 are reclaimable, with up to 50% for those who are older, while there are £1,500 grants for taking on an apprentice.

The new online 'levy' of large employers promised by government to be delivered next year by a new IT system for new apprentice qualifications is surely a recipe for complete opacity! Meanwhile, most apprentice training continues to be restricted to narrow workplace-based NVQs, with functional skills added on for those without A-C GCSE maths and English. In this respect, the UK system is unlike that in other European countries where some form of classroom-based education is provided (in Germany, for example, where apprentices attend college courses).

In Germany, rather than just being linked to a particular job, completing an apprenticeship gives a young person a 'licence to practice' a particular trade or occupation. German apprenticeship management and organisation are also the product of a 'social partnership' between the local state, trade unions and employers, who are legally required to provide apprenticeships. Again, this is a very different situation to the UK where the decision whether to provide an apprenticeship is left to individual employers. The disappearance of many technical and 'middling jobs' – as described in Chapter Three – means most UK employers don't really need apprentices, and this is the reason why most don't offer them. Despite the pick-up in apprenticeship starts by young people (as above), until recently the government's own statistics pointed to an overall fall in numbers (see Richard, 2012).

However, as seen in this chapter, there is cross-party consensus on the need for apprenticeships as part of a vocational route for 'those who are not academic but want to do something practical', as it is often patronisingly put. Apprenticeships have the appeal of John Major's 'Modern Apprenticeships' that sounded simultaneously modern and reassuringly traditional. They are also something that many parents, teachers, policy-makers and school leavers desperately want to believe in, as they often do in the power of education. They also have the appeal to policy-makers and pundits of a 'magic solution', conjuring 'engineers, accountants and project managers' out of the ground, so that bringing back apprenticeships will miraculously turn the English service economy back into a productive German one, just as bringing back grammar schools will restart upward social mobility. Yet the fact that applications for overpriced and often insubstantial undergraduate degrees have held up in the way that they have is an indication that young people and their parents have not been so bamboozled as to think that most apprenticeships offer any better hopes of the secure, at least semi-professional, employment that most young people aspire to.

## Summary

This chapter has shown that the attempted 'great reversal' (Allen and Ainley, 2013a) in education policy under the coalition was a response to Labour's 'education, education, education', summarised in Chapter One. Seeking to reclaim 'standards' and heighten distinctions between learners, it was intended to restore a new correspondence between education, qualifications and the labour market in a situation of declining employment opportunities for young people. It has not succeeded in doing so, and although the outcomes of the examination changes outlined for schools are not yet clear, the growing loss of legitimacy in education and apprenticeships without jobs demands alternatives. These are discussed in the final chapter, where proposals for changes to education are presented. These are advanced as part of a more general economic and social strategy to improve the lives of young people and to resolve the generational crisis of society.

# FIVE

# A new politics of education

A main theme of this book has been that despite the gospel of salvation through education, changes in work and occupations have increased inequality and reduced the certainty of employment. For the majority of the younger generation this has led to a serious mismatch between employment opportunities and their educational qualifications, expectations and aspirations. Instead of 'moving up', many young people face the possibility of downward mobility into low-paid, low-skilled employment, so that the risk of being 'underemployed' is at least as great as being unemployed. Chapter One recounted the history of how this happened. Chapter Two pointed to the increase in low-skilled, low-paid jobs at the expense of managerial and professional high-paid ones. Chapter Three saw this as reflected in a 'pear-shaped' occupational structure, with the majority of people 'pushed down' rather than 'pulled up'. Chapter Four described the consequences for schools and universities where the mass of students find themselves running up a down-escalator.

This chapter suggests specific policy responses as well as indicating a general way forward. It begins by considering what can be done about widening access to all levels of learning, and stressing the importance of preventing further divisive academic selection. The block put on progress by England's uniquely dominant private schools is acknowledged. With little practicable to be done immediately about these, this chapter looks briefly at an alternative approach from the National Union of Teachers (NUT) as an instance of a new democratic professionalism. This is contrasted with traditional politics of education, questioning its habitual demands for teacher training, qualification reform and local authority control. Instead, a new youth politics is anticipated, and the record of demonstration and riot is briefly reviewed, as well as the reactions of other campaigning groups to youth demands.

Foremost among these is advocacy of the abolition of world record level undergraduate fees. (This will be no more expensive than the money wasted through their non-repayment.) Further education needs to be saved before it is too late, and regional linkages established to recreated colleges by schools and universities to limit academic competition and institutional differentiation. This, in turn, relates to regional regeneration of a diversified economy, taking as many 18+-year-olds as possible on through a school leaving diploma to further study and/or training to opportunities for employment. Recognising that technological change potentially enables a variety of occupations throughout an individual's working life, this chapter asks what constitutes an appropriate general educational entitlement for a democratic and sustainable society. This is the central question with which this book confronts its reader.

## Towards a democratic professionalism

Teachers and lecturers who keep the show on the road every day in schools, colleges and universities have been demoralised by the 'discourse of derision' (Ball, 2012) directed particularly at school teachers by successive government ministers. This adds to the feeling of loss of legitimacy they sense all around them, but they can't see how to get themselves out of the corners they have been boxed into, save by leaving the profession – four in ten in their first qualified year in schools, according to a 2015 survey by the Association of Teachers and Lecturers. Many other entrants are put off by the stultified Ofsted-led training. The result is a serious shortage of teachers. Those who struggle on are caught in various double-binds so that, for instance, no teacher is going to say they are not in favour of 'raising standards' or of 'accountability'. Yet agreeing to these seemingly reasonable requests implies still more targets that are set only to be failed, together with still more inspection and monitoring. Many teachers know this is not in the best interests of those they teach, who are their first concern.

By contrast, for most of the postwar period, the main issue for progressive educationalists was widening and democratising access. This was part of a more general push for equal opportunities where genuine advances were made. This should continue to be an important activity, as inequalities in education are increased by current government policies. For example, it is vital to campaign against the extension of grammar schools, forced academisation and 'free schools' that have been shown to heighten inequalities, and to argue for such schools to be returned to locally democratically controlled education authorities in preference to chains of charities. As argued in Chapter Four, different types of schools with different types of admission policies only intensify the competition to get a place at 'a good school' (for which read 'a good crammer'), and amplify the reduction of education to a 'positional good', valued in 'exchange' not in use.

To purchase such a positional good can be seen to be the purpose of private schools for those who can afford to pay to send their children to them. They present an uneven profile from small and specialist to large and lavishly endowed. In the latter, it is not surprising that they can instil habits of often arrogant confidence in their pupils, while their academic provision benefits from low class sizes but amounts to cramming in too many cases. Pressure should be maintained to abolish their charitable status, but if this turned into a prolonged legal minefield, there should also be pressure to restrict their powers of influence compared with state schools, in particular, the close connections of 'the great public schools' with the 'antique' universities, perverting any pretence of equal access from the top down. But progressive education politics has to move beyond concern solely with access, which any opposition is at present powerless to do anything about other than expose exclusion and the contradiction with the ideology of social mobility through education that such privilege implies.

As an example of a different approach, prior to the general election the NUT produced *A manifesto for our children's education* (2014). It went beyond the usual rhetoric about the importance of education for the economy, instead highlighting themes from reform of the curriculum to the need to restore local democratic control over schools. This was a bold initiative, very different from the postwar period when the NUT acted as the 'voice of the profession', operating as a powerful lobbying organisation that had the ear of the Secretary of State. Those days are long gone and now, embroiled in a protracted battle to maintain national pay and working conditions which has involved a series of strikes, the Union has recognised the importance of mobilising members around popular alternative education policies, and developing a campaigning style aimed at winning support from parents and other sections of the communities that schools serve. The NUT is also at the forefront of campaigning against the government's new anti-union legislation, as well as defending schools against continuing cuts in resources which, despite ring-fencing, are steadily depreciating while demographic and other demands on state schools pile up.

This reaction from England's largest teachers' union is part of a new public sector unionism that recognises in the crisis of social democracy that parliamentary representatives can no longer be relied on to secure reforms on the unions' behalf. So, faced with relentless onslaught, unions have to defend themselves. For teachers and lecturers it is also part of a new 'democratic professionalism' that builds on professional collegiality to contest the proletarianisation of teaching in schools, colleges and universities. This reduction to the condition of waged labour has prompted trade union organisation, which is now denser among professional groups than among many manual workers, and more extensive in the public than in the private sector.

Teachers and lecturers are thus likely to find themselves alongside other public sector workers who are being or soon will be subjected by the Conservative government to the same treatment – civil servants, doctors, lawyers, nurses, social workers and others (see Lethbridge,

2015). Together with craft and other mainly manual workers concentrated in surviving transport and other industries that are still well unionised, professions old and new find themselves resisting the same pressures from management. New technology is applied across the board to break down the expertise of communities of practice into itemised and interchangeable tasks for individual assessment by performance-related pay in outsourced and downsized disorganisations.

Education and training has a key role in the creation and maintenance of such communities of professional and craft practice, but education is losing legitimacy as the opportunities to apply acquired knowledge and skills are being lost. As a result, learning at all levels becomes merely the rehearsal of performance, in what Lave and McDermott (2002) called 'estranged learning'. Collective cultures that are critically acquired through education to be adapted to their own use by future generations are being picked apart. The tyranny of transparency of McArdle-Clinton's 2008 'capsule education' breaks them down for behavioural assessment and itemised quantification, "practising what exactly to write and where in preparation for exams", as the student quoted in Chapter Four said.

This insidious process is not recognised by the old professional associations seeking to maintain their influence over educational politics, like the New Visions Group, for instance, whose invited membership includes senior education academics and administrators, headteachers and well-known figures from parents', governors' and teachers' organisations. But far from a 'new vision', they are essentially seeking to renegotiate the old postwar settlement referred to above and in Chapter One, and in particular, to restore the influence of professional educators within it. They have been profoundly unsettled by the election of Jeremy Corbyn to Labour's leadership, but in many ways their mindset is shared by many of the new activists.

For instance, at the heart of this traditional politics of education is the idea that the major problem is that education has been hijacked by right-wing or neoliberal forces that have had a disastrous effect on 'our schools' so that they need to be 'reclaimed'. The area where the loss of professional control is most keenly felt is teacher training. The government has shifted this back towards an apprentice model of the worst purely imitative and uncritical sort in the schools where it started in Victorian times. This was before teacher training graduated to trade training in teacher colleges of FE that eventually associated themselves with HE. Here teacher education – as it briefly became – was turned into competence- or 'standards'-based teacher training now under the direct inspection of Ofsted as part of what has been suggested is becoming an extended further and higher/tertiary education sector.

The demand for 'qualified teachers' therefore needs rethinking if their only qualification is certification in delivering Ofsted-imposed competences by sorting children into HAPs, MAPs and LAPs, or whatever other policy the government proposes that goes against the professional judgement of older teachers whose experience is being lost. For example, in teaching the so-called 'funny phonics' reading method that may have actually hampered primary pupils' acquisition of literacy. Recent resistance supported by parents to 'baseline tests' for four-year-olds is an apt response by early years practitioners in infant schools.

Instead of aiming to build democratic professionalism, however, qualification reform is a favourite preoccupation of traditional educational politics. Indeed, this chapter endorses a general diploma of school graduation below! However, at least it recognises that this is only a start, which by itself is not going to significantly alter social mobility flows without change also to the structure of opportunities. And yet, as Ken Roberts concludes in his *Class in modern Britain* (2001, p 224), 'virtually all policy-makers and many sociologists continue to act as if modest interventions in education and training will bring about significant redistribution of life-chances.'

Another example of a habitual demand is to return schools to local authority control, which is a reflex response of Corbynite Labour, dovetailing with what seems to be the waiting game being played by the Campaign for State Education/Local Schools Network. This demand does not recognise that LEAs hardly exist as they used to, especially when they have become Departments of Children's Services and councils have also been freighted with responsibilities for delivering care in the community. Starved of resources, local councils are reduced towards a core of highly paid accountants overseen by councillors on expanded living allowances deciding which of various private tenderers to pick to deliver services at the lowest possible rate to the dwindling turn-out at local elections. Worcestershire County Council, for instance, has recently tendered all its schools out for delivery by Babcock International Engineering Support Services Plc (motto: 'Working diligently behind the scenes'), which has immediately proposed cutting teaching assistants and special needs provision.

Still, it has to be admitted that the public at large, and even most parents, do not seem to care much about who provides schooling. This indifference is at odds with the education gospel, and points to the limits of its legitimacy as academic education comes to be cynically seen by all concerned as a game, as irrelevant to most people's lives as the old secondary modern schooling most people left at the earliest opportunity. Old-style professional politics only reinforce the postwar assumptions about education as a reformer and leveller that were always limited but which today no longer apply. It is thus largely ignorant of the changed relationship between education and the occupational order. On the contrary, it prioritises 'learning for its own sake' and an education that encourages young people to participate in society.

In themselves these are laudable aims, but emphasising a 'love of learning' at the expense of everything else sidesteps the arguments outlined earlier. It ignores the fact that increased participation in education has been the result of the collapse of the postwar model of transition and the disappearance of 'youth jobs'. As has been made clear, the real crisis is a creeping loss of legitimacy for education. Instead of enabling young people to *get on*, even highly qualified young people find it increasingly difficult to *get by*. As stated in the Introduction, for young people, education and employment are closely related, and a failure to provide the latter limits what can be achieved by the former. This is seen in the struggle of schools to achieve results in areas of persisting high unemployment, not so much because of deprivation as because of lack of future prospects to apply learning. The old professionalist model of education politics refuses to recognise such connections, and insists that 'teacher knows best', ignoring the need for 'the educators to be educated'. This is the reason why its initiatives receive little support from defrauded youth.

## And a new youth politics

One group missing from such education campaigns on their behalf is young people themselves. To an extent this reflects a situation where there is no major national youth organisation able to articulate their demands, although the Campaign Against Fees and Cuts is an independent movement drawing on activists in and out of the NUS to call large demonstrations and university occupations. The NUS itself seeks to represent apprentices as well as FE and HE students and used to speak for sixth formers. In winter 2010-11, the trebling of English undergraduate fees provoked large university student demonstrations, joined in spring 2011 by sixth form and FE college students protesting the loss of their Educational Maintenance Allowances (EMAs). Months later, young people again took to the streets, this time in the inner cities. These two groups of student protesters and urban rioters, rather than representing a new 'precariat' emerging as a 'class for itself', in the way Guy Standing suggested, are two very different constituencies that it is difficult to bring together for long. This is despite the fact that they often live in the same inner-city neighbourhoods, ducking and diving at the same part-time 'McJobs'.

On the one hand, the urban rioters – *The Guardian* estimating that almost 80% of those up in court were under 25 (12 August 2012) – have become marginal to society. Failed by an academic testing regime and dropping out of 'participation' from the age of 14 on, without work and without hope, they no longer play by any rules. Not having any commitment to 'fairness' or any faith in 'social justice', they have been cast into youth's new so-called 'underclass'. Not 'political' compared to the students, but according to some Manchester youngsters interviewed by BBC News (11 August 2011), the riots were 'the best protest ever' against a system that denied them access to the consumer goods they saw flaunted around them.

On the other hand, the student protestors could be identified as middle or 'aspirational' working class. They were the children of what has been described as a working middle/middle working class. They had played by the rules and worked hard at school, but quickly became politicised in response to the way HE was being put out of their reach and that of their younger brothers and sisters. Their sudden awareness subsided just as quickly as it had arisen, so that the academics who had supported them no longer rely on a student movement to sustain an escalating 'resistance', as Bailey and Freedman hoped in 2011. The brief efflorescence of the student 'springtime' (Solomon and Palmieri, 2011) left only the eloquent Campaign for the Defence of the Public University (Holmwood, 2012), alongside the more august but possibly for that reason more effective Council for the Defence of British Universities. Neither of these academic organisations involves students to any extent.

For its part, the University and College Union (UCU) declares its determination to fight on a case-by-case basis the inevitable course closures and redundancies that have already begun in HE, and that have been going on in FE for the past 30 years. Beyond this tactical response, the Union's general strategy is informed by an acceptance of the doubtful notion of a 'knowledge economy' critiqued in Chapter Two. UCU thus seeks to show government and the public that universities and colleges should be subsidised for their contribution to a multi-billion export industry, and for producing 'information workers' for the domestic economy.

This brings us to the nub of the matter, as the traditional politics of education similarly seeks to present qualification reform as a way to return to vocational learning for work but this time on a parity of esteem with academic cramming for university. Tedious though the latter is, it continues to be preferred by students as a route to such secure employment as remains. By comparison, the vocational route remains an inferior option that leads nowhere, as trades and crafts collapse into digitised outsourcing and the peripheral labour model.

Overall, there is no coordinated response by parents, teachers and students across all schools, colleges and universities to the changes being inflicted on state education at all levels, and perhaps this is too much to hope for at this stage. However, it is the aim to which we should aspire to create a joined-up National Education Service, as Jeremy Corbyn suggests rebadging it, and it is the overview presented here since it affords the completest understanding of education and training in relation to the state, economy and society.

## Education in the 'second machine age'

Although transformation of the occupational structure is not directly determined by technology, in free market societies, where the accumulation of economic power goes largely unchecked, owners and investors will always have the last word over how and where to use new technologies to increase output. As a result, for Erik Brynjolfsson and Andrew McAfee (2014), the 'second machine age' is likely to have serious implications for employment and inequality. To begin with, digital technologies facilitate an infinite increase in output without incurring a counteracting increase in costs necessary to produce more goods and services. So, whereas the increases in production associated with the first machine age of industrial production resulted in the creation of a 'mass' workforce, the new digital corporations require only a tiny fraction of these. Facebook for example, as Brynjolfsson and McAfee relate, although having almost a billion average daily users, an annual turnover approaching US$13 billion and a net income of nearly US$3 billion, employs only 9,199 people. This strengthens the trend towards super-rich 'stars and superstars' who are Dorling's 0.1%, or Picketty's 'super managers'. So there is further polarisation, pulling those at the very top away from those in what used to be an affluent 'middle' – the bureaucracy of managers and administrators who serviced the Fordist mass production era.

How far non-routine work can be automated is part of a wider debate about the potential of robotic technology. Mass media advertising endlessly unveils the latest in long lines of personalised gizmos, pushing the technological boundaries to undertake a multiplicity of both domestic and workplace tasks. Brynjolfsson and

McAfee accept that there will always be activities that even the most intelligent machines find difficult, from 'walking up stairs' to 'picking up a paper clip' and that, unlike machines, humans have the imagination to innovate. It is still the case, however, that 'digital machines have escaped their narrow confines and started to demonstrate broad abilities in pattern recognition, complex communication and other domains that used to be exclusively human' (Brynjolfsson and McAfee, 2014, p 91). Ironically, however, the fact that wages continue to fall and, as Chapters Two and Three have noted, the supply of labour available for unskilled work appears inexhaustible, may – at least for a time – put a brake on the complete subordination of labour to the machine. Note, for example, the way that manual car washes have reappeared staffed by immigrant labour in place of the automated ones on every garage forecourt a few years ago (an example borrowed from Clark and Heath, 2014, pp 90-1).

Brynjolfsson and McAfee are aware of the potential downsides, both social and psychological, of universal digitisation. Nevertheless, they advocate a NewsCorp/Pearson diet of MOOCs and teaching machines in schools of the type that Michael Gove was so keen on – until the phone-hacking scandal curtailed his many private meetings with Rupert Murdoch! That this will produce the entrepreneurs of the future, putting together the latest applications of new technologies, shared freely across the World Wide Web to become market leaders in a blaze of creative destruction, is clearly more magical thinking.

But Brynjolfsson and McAfee's critique of, if not their solution to, the practices of what should be considered 'Fordist'/first machine age' education is surely a valid one. As has been argued previously (Ainley and Allen, 2010), instead of spending hours sitting in rows, being schooled by their teachers, young people in the later secondary years especially should surely use their abilities with the new technologies in 'really personal learning' (p 151). Teachers and lecturers would then be valued for their skills as 'tutors' or 'mentors', even co-investigators and co-creators – not just as 'deliverers' of Gove's top-down, neo-academic, grammar school National Curriculum.

It is reasonable to assume that for those under 14, schooling would remain a largely formal experience, if a much less regimented and more creative one, in non-selective and non-denominational schools without uniforms, and involving more discussion and debate in place of perpetual exam prep (see, for example, Coultas, 2013, on making meaning in secondary English, and Waugh, 2015, similarly, in adult education). Learning can then be more self-directed to make it much more interesting and enjoyable. It can also be more collaborative, with shared projects and productions requiring innovative approaches to assessment other than individually 'under exam conditions'. As well as continuing to interact with fellow students in the way described below, online learning can afford the creation of a variety of communities of learning in new forums for the exchange of different ideas.

To encourage this approach, the ubiquitous bureaucracies 'driving up standards' by ticking the electronic boxes of the new 'responsive and flexible learning systems' can be dismantled. They would not be missed – especially Ofsted! The army of quality controllers who have carved out careers as part of the 'leadership' culture designed to support schools as business units seeking to meet 'outcomes', not to mention the battalions of private sector 'consultants', could be more effectively employed directly supporting young people. Teachers need to take these matters back into their own hands in collaboration with their students.

Certainly, the whole expensive and overloaded exams and tests industry needs trimming back before it grows even more unreliable and dysfunctional, especially as all this emphasis on 'kwality' (as Ted Wragg, 'the teachers' friend', writing in *The Times Education Supplement* used to call it) encourages 'gaming' to meet key targets, and notoriously fails to prevent plagiarism and plain cheating by students and teachers alike. Nor has it allayed suspicions of widespread 'dumbing down' (in the politically incorrect phrase) rather than 'wising up'. The point is often made that a huge amount of resources could be redeployed if the prime function of education was stimulating learning, not quantifying and measuring it!

But in becoming tutors and facilitators, without being relegated to instructors and demonstrators, teaching as a whole would require a new professional culture, in particular, more egalitarian relationships with students in place of the current rigidly hierarchical relationships between teachers and taught. The 'deschooling' philosophy of Ivan Illich (1971), for example, could be reconsidered not so as to dismantle schools and colleges, but to reconstitute them as community centres. So, too, the 'informal education' advanced by Tony Jeffs and Mark Smith in 1990 need no longer be confined to youth workers and community educators employed outside the classroom.

## A good general education for everybody

The changes in the nature of work and occupations described in Chapters Two and Three, together with future possibilities outlined in this chapter, means there is even less reason for ranking academically examined so-called 'powerful knowledge' over 'alternative' vocational qualifications. However, these are no longer appropriate for the diminishing number of intermediate-level occupations, so instead, a new 'general diploma' should be established as the main qualification after the age of 14. A general high school graduation diploma at 18, linked to the assumption of citizenship as in the US, would provide entitlement to different forms of learning beyond foundational schooling, just as apprenticeships are regarded as an entitlement in Germany, not as a relegation route, as they are here. This would recognise high-quality technical education and training undertaken at school, in college or on work placements, so that 'learning about work', not just 'learning to work', would be part of a common core. Such a common curriculum entitlement would also nurture talents towards expertise through different types of learning –from discussion and working in groups on creative arts projects to scientific investigations, sports, dance, music and other recreations.

Given the existing sorry state of affairs, this level of change and innovation, basic and obvious though it sounds, could not happen all at once. The first stage would have to be an overarching certificate linking the different types of existing qualifications. Tomlinson's proposals to integrate academic and vocational learning into a common framework including A-levels, rejected by Blair in 2005, are a precedent for this first step. If this were to serve as a bridge towards more radical changes, however, subject combinations would need to be considerably more prescriptive than those outlined in previous reform blueprints.

Completing the general diploma would also entitle access to HE for those that wanted it. The current unequal competition for students and research grants between mass universities for the many and elite universities for the few should be replaced by a regional infrastructure in which first priority would be given to local applicants, many living at home as in mainland Europe and Scotland. Everyone aged 18 or older should be entitled to grant funding towards living costs financed in the absence of tuition fees, which should be abolished. Since so many loans for fees and maintenance will never be recovered, this would not incur any additional expense, and might even save money. The Labour Party's policy at the last general election to reduce fees was a step in the right direction, even if 'fees are only the half of it' (Ainley, 2015).

Of course, not everyone wants to go to university – including many of those who are already there! – and the competition to get in has the effect of sifting students according to their parental background by levels of academic literacy. The different discourses they acquire in arts and humanities degrees in turn affect their entry to the hierarchy of 'graduatised' employment. Nevertheless, they are distinguished from non-graduate entry jobs to which the other 'half our future' (HMSO, 1963), with inferior vocational or no qualifications, are relegated.

Instead of this tertiary-level correspondence with the labour market between the academic and the vocational, the vocational nature of HE should be recognised as extending to the most prestigious of subjects at the most elite institutions, as in the 'original vocations' of law and medicine. This includes an academic vocation dedicated to learning critically from the past to inform change in the future. All undergraduates should be aware that they will be expected to make some contribution to that continuing cultural conversation as the final degree demonstration of their graduation. Such development will widen the still available critical space afforded by HE in which a defence of the public university can be conducted (Holmwood, 2012). This will bring together staff and students, not antagonise them, which is the effect of putting customers/students at the heart of the system, as the BIS (2011) White Paper claimed to do.

General education in schools should also be informed by the discussion, research and scholarship preserved and developed in post-compulsory further, higher and adult continuing education. This is a process of critically transmitting culture down the generations, including artistic creation and physical recreation, invention and discovery. As suggested, a general diploma at 18 (since this is now the current 'participation age') should thus be available for everybody along the lines of the US high school graduation model. This would contribute towards preventing the social isolation of an 'underclass', like Scottish highers at 17, which have helped a larger proportion of school leavers into FE and HE in all the time that England was sorting pupils into CSEs and O-levels. Additional specialisation into science or humanities A-levels was famously criticised by C.P. Snow in 1959 for sustaining 'two cultures' that need to be unified, but the current Education Secretary, Nicky Morgan, repeatedly advocates it.

Fundamentally, the perception of 'the problem' needs to shift from the fixation on better preparing young people for 'employability' by providing 'pre-vocational' school, FE or HE, or through government-backed pseudo-work placements, bogus apprenticeships and interminable internships. An alternative economic framework of job creation in which local authorities and public/voluntary sector alliances generate employment opportunities is required. Following the Green Party, this should be a diversified economy. Without this, changes to apprenticeship funding, proposed by Richard in 2012, contributed – as Martin Allen predicted (in Allen and Ainley, 2014, p 19) – to a reduction in the number of apprentices, although quantity if not quality have since been boosted.

Given the intensification of the 'low skill equilibrium' first related by Finegold and Soskice in 1988 to the deregulated, post-industrial, largely service-based economy of the UK, repeated efforts to cajole and bribe employers into subscribing to training and apprenticeships they do not want or need are wasted. Ever since the collapse of industrial apprenticeships, rebuilding a vocational route with 'parity of esteem' to the traditional academic one has been a lost cause. From the first raising of the school leaving age in 1972, through the sorry history of youth training (Ainley, 1988), to widening participation to HE, this has functioned to sustain illusions in worthless vocational qualifications (Wolf, 2011).

Within HE by contrast, vocational subjects such as law and medicine have always been oversubscribed by those who are qualified, but young people sign up in their thousands for newer areas like business studies, which now attracts 10% of all applications and equals about 20% plus of all HE students. In 'the business studies university' (see Ainley, 2016: forthcoming), students of other subjects also undertake more or less compulsory modules tacked onto their programmes of study, supplementing them with various aspects of what can be called 'BS', such as marketing or business organisation, for example, 'entrepreneurialism', or the 'employability' that is as omnipresent here as elsewhere.

A high level of applications for courses that are perceived to be directly vocational is understandable given the available alternatives and the increases in student fees. However, the definition of a graduate-level job has become ever more elastic as this is a key indicator on which funding for universities depends (more 'gaming'). Ironically, this is worse for the supposedly more vocationally inclined post-1994 universities, but also includes many students who opt for science and technology subjects at other institutions. They often find that, to avoid relegation to technician-level lab work, they have to proceed to postgraduation. This is further turning still larger parts of HE into FE, and squeezing what remains of FE engineering, for instance, out of FE and into HE, as employers prefer graduates to 'apprentices' for increasingly routinised technical work. At the same time, 'high-flying' graduate employers continue to recruit more from a small number of elite institutions than they do from specific subject disciplines.

Raised and differentiated tuition fees can only increase this commodification of student experience and heighten distinctions between students and between their HE institutions, as well as between 'students' and 'apprentices'. Reductions in fees are necessary, but there should also be an emphasis on the contribution to knowledge that students can make in their chosen field of study. In this way, HE can recover itself in connection with further training to build a 'thick HE', one that is both theoretically informed and practically competent. This involves thinking through what a general schooling of the type sketched above could contribute to 'fully developed individuals, fit for a variety of labours, ready to face any change of production, and to whom the different social functions they perform, are but so many modes of giving free scope to their own natural and acquired powers' (Marx, 1971, p 494). This is the ideal of a general intellect that could be fostered in comprehensive schools and developed throughout a democratic society.

## Socially useful education

In 1975, just as new information and communications technology (ICT) was beginning to be applied to complex manufacturing processes, Mike Cooley chaired the Lucas Aerospace Combine Shop Stewards' Committee. This created the Lucas Workers' Plan for Socially Useful Production when the Anglo-French consortium stopped making the Concorde aeroplane. Cooley aimed to avoid 'repeating in the field of intellectual work ... the mistakes made ... at an earlier historical stage' in the first industrial revolution when 'skilled manual work... was subjected to the use of high-capital equipment' (1987, p 9). Cooley therefore wanted 'human-centred technology' to guide mechanical automation.

Thirty years later, as new ICT was becoming diffused throughout society but with millennial hopes still high that this could recombine theory with practice in FE colleges as the new polytechnics, the Principal of Lewisham College, Ruth Silver, suggested to a meeting in the House of Commons that, at the same time as students at

Lewisham's partner Universities of Greenwich, Goldsmiths and South Bank aimed higher, they should also go further. By attending Lewisham College they could acquire the practical competences employers always complain are missing in graduates who have only theoretical 'book knowledge' without practical application. This was not to denigrate 'lower-level' training, but to recognise that 'higher-level' education is impossible without it, whereas it is quite possible – and increasingly common – to have training without education, for example, in today's teacher training. What Silver called 'thick HE' would thus unite practical competence with generalised knowledge. Unfortunately the idea never caught on!

A similar socially useful education is now required. Creating it would be an education in itself for those teacher trade unions and other associations, including those of parents and students who might be involved in the process. Together with Martin Allen, I made a start towards such a project with the 2013 book that we edited called *Education beyond the coalition* (Allen and Ainley, 2013b). This collected chapters covering all sectors of education from primary to postgraduate schools, proposing practical alternatives to the existing situation in their respective areas. While these did not add up to a coherent programme across education as a whole, they did suggest ways forward in each of their fields of education, and left their integration open to further development and discussion.

For FE, for example, Robin Simmons (2014) urged a return to the integrative principles of the 1980 Macfarlane report. This had recommended 16+ tertiary colleges, but was rejected by the Thatcher government despite the economies of scale that would have followed. Instead, government underfunding and the competition between colleges to run ever-lower level and often virtualised courses now threatens the viability of the sector (see Wolf, 2015). This is a problem some in government wish would just go away – as Hodgson and Spours recount (2015, p 204): 'Vince Cable's revelation that DBIS officials proposed FE colleges be abolished to save money and no one would notice.' It is a view shared by many in HE! Despite current closures and mergers across 'areas', FE cannot be made to disappear so easily, with perhaps five million full- and part-time students and trainees, depending how you count them. And FE and HE (or TE) remains a potential lynchpin around which to reorganise a learning infrastructure linked to local and regional economies in what Spours and Hodgson called, in 2012, 'a unified ecosystem vision' of schools and colleges in relation to universities.

As it is, although halved in number since being freed from local authority control as independently competing corporations in 1993, the FE sector still constitutes a diverse range of institutions: 244 general FE colleges, 94 sixth form colleges, 15 specialist designated institutions, over 1,000 private or charitable training providers, over 200 public bodies such as local authorities offering community learning, 38 HE institutions also offering FE courses, 18 national skills academies, and the training departments of major employers such as Rolls-Royce, NHS trusts and government departments such as the Ministry of Defence, Prison Service and Armed Services (Lingfield, 2012). Despite this breadth and variety, 16-19 education is funded at £4,000 annually per full-time equivalent student, compared with £5,000 in schools and £9,000 per undergraduate. Only adults fare worse, with the Adult Skills Budget to colleges cut by 40% in the last Parliament as government sought to increase numbers of 'apprentices' (Playfair, 2015). Meanwhile, as shown, FE is being decanted into HE, including the sixth form colleges and college centres that have lost out to government-favoured school sixth forms.

Despite all this, further and continuing adult education retains (at least historically) an ideal of education that is comprehensive without being uniform. Like youth work, provision in the colleges was not necessarily vocationally related, but could also be re-creative or rehabilitative. Indeed, Bill Bailey and I recorded in 1997 that it was important to the professional identity of the FE lecturers we interviewed that colleges (unlike schools) never failed anybody and (unlike universities) never turned anybody away. Instead, a place was found for students in a range of provision from entry to postgraduate level, with everything in between. Whatever their starting point, students could progress (if they were able and wished to do so) without fear of failure. So, while employers continue to demand government subsidies for general training they are unwilling to provide in-house because of their perennial fear of 'poaching' from each other in an unregulated market, FE maintains its potential – to support apprenticeships, for instance, despite the current distortions of placing students in colleges as holding pens to hide unemployment and of 'learningfare' courses that they have to attend as a condition of receiving benefits.

To reanimate the ideal of the FE colleges, as of the US community colleges (Harbour, 2015), would involve academic teachers in sixth forms and universities forsaking the sacerdotal role bestowed on them by the education gospel, epitomised earlier as 'teacher knows best'. At the same time, teachers' constant inability to fulfil the promises of the gospel results only in their further scapegoating through Ball's 'discourse of derision', as more impossible demands are heaped on them. It is often difficult, too, for pupils/students to see past the promises that structure their 'learning journeys', and many have a personal investment in not doing so. At the same time, running up the down-escalator to stay in the same place saps the legitimacy of learning, reducing it to an elaborate charade that is becoming increasingly transparent.

In fact, 'bullshit detection', proposed by Postman and Weingartner as essential to 'teaching as a subversive activity' (1969), should be the central activity of education at all levels – not just in the 'criticality' routinely demanded in HE. Everyone needs to know 'how to see through the hype, spin and lies of modern life' (Glaser, 2012). Critical literacy is, as Phil Beadle writes in one of his 'How to teach' books, that are each worth a thousand Ofsted observations, 'a matter of life and death for working-class people':

> … it is the path away from the black economy and the hand-to-mouth existence that condemns millions of decent people to lives of misery and debt. With literacy, you can fight the policy makers who have never seen close up what poverty can do to humans, who legislate to increase it, who seek to put its victims under a pathologising miscroscope and then blame them

for some innate, probably genetic, failing; when the failing has been inflicted upon them by politics and circumstance.

It is not endorsing the education gospel to say with Beadle that, 'With literacy you can articulate your anger' (2015, p 11).

Through informed and critical discussion, students and teachers at all levels of learning can come to a shared understanding of what is going on. It is surely a little remarked tragedy that the majority of the population of this country are unable, as well as often unwilling, to read a broadsheet newspaper from cover to cover so as to follow a sustained written argument, let alone enjoy a classic novel. Consequently, most discussion is conducted above their heads by others on their behalf, a situation to which most people have long inured themselves.

The Bullock Report (HMSO, 1975) was the last major government effort to attempt to address this literacy lack and to reassert the reforming ideal of education leading to social change. It drew on the work of Bernstein with an emphasis on language across the curriculum. Such an approach would again have to be adopted to really raise levels of reading and communication generally, not one-off rival campaigns sponsored by Royals and other worthies occasionally reading to primary children. Every schoolteacher will agree with Martell's generalisation in *The politics of reading and writing*, 'As you move down the socio-economic class scale, kids read and write less well' (1976, p 107).

Obviously, all teachers want the best for their students and to help them as far as they can – not just because their own security of employment and pay can depend on their performance! Yet teachers in universities no less than in schools and colleges are put in a double-bind as increasing students' reliance on guidance and direction makes them less able to take the risks of mistakes and misunderstanding necessarily involved in learning. The few subjects like sociology, where it is possible to talk about the situation that students and teachers share so as to confront it directly, are being squeezed from the school curriculum and sidelined in HE. Others, like economics, are confined to neoliberal orthodoxy – although there are moves against this with the development of heterodox economics started by University of Manchester students and even of critical management studies (see, for example, Alvesson, 2013).

The unrealistically too 'great expectations' of education to transform society and restart social mobility are acknowledged on all sides, but are not fully explored or explained, as this book has tried to do. Building on this often uneasy recognition, however, it is possible to go further in discussion, sometimes around the edges of official learning tasks. Students can then be afforded opportunities to understand themselves as part of a social situation which is not of their own making and for which they cannot be blamed, but for which they may see new alternatives. Ultimately these will be political and economic, but the starting point should be one of entitlement. This is not necessarily 'the right to work' under which the traditional left harks back to a postwar collectivised model of the labour market. Rather, the right not to work might be raised in the form of a Citizen's Income. This has been proposed (by Gorz and Standing, for example) to address the current situation in which there are more people in the workforce but they are paid less for unregulated employment. It is not as if there is not work to be done and, as indicated, a green economy will necessarily be a labour-intensive as well as a diverse one (see CACC, 2010). If the ecological challenges are to be met, it is coming to be appreciated that they will require international mobilisation unparalleled in peacetime.

Education at every level should therefore contribute to building the skills and knowledge to best apply the latest technological developments to socially useful advantage. Through the expertise it develops, it should also play more of a part in informing the debate over what is socially useful (Collins, 2014). This discussion can begin by recognising how new technology has been applied during economic restructuring under the new market state to deskill so many of the tasks involved in production, distribution and services. It can also address the consequent closure and control inflicted on the minds of pupils and students, realising that this is a shared situation in which teachers, too, are implicated. Investigation, experiment, creation and debate by as many people as possible is vital to preserving and extending the remaining 'critical space' within education.

Integrating scientific research, technical craft, scholarship and artistry at all levels of learning would not deny the need also for specialist research. This should be dedicated to contributing solutions to ecological and other crises, and not prostituted to immediate commercial 'impact'.

To preserve critical space and to counter 'dumbing down' in the reduction of education to training, to reverse privatisation of public service education and maintain free provision requires a new direction at all levels. Education can then remain true to the Enlightenment ideal of understanding in order to control society, and so adapt it to its natural environment. Humanity faces again the old alternative of 'socialism or barbarism', now posed in terms of human survival. As President Obama repeated, borrowing from the previous year's conference on sea-level rise, 'We are the first generation to feel the effects of climate change, and the last generation that can do something about it' (*The Week*, 23 September 2014).

## A crisis for youth, not a skills crisis

This book has outlined major changes to the labour market that make the 'transition' from education to the workplace and from youth to adulthood much more prolonged, uncertain and precarious, changing the nature of both youth and adulthood (Silva, 2015). This is reflected in the fact that 21% of 25- to 29-year-olds and 8% of 30- to 34-year-olds continue to live with their parents (ONS, 21 January 2014b). Not so long ago they would have established families of their own while approaching their peak earnings in occupations enabling them to find independent housing and contribute to pensions. That so many are now unable to do this indicates a crisis for society that will predictably find future generations worse off than their parents.

Refuting claims that young people's inability to progress is the result of a lack of education or skills, it has been argued to the contrary that education now plays an important role in excluding young people from the labour market so that approximately one in three of *all* 18- to 24-year-olds are recorded as being in full-time education or training (see Table A06, ONS Labour Market Bulletin, March 2015, which also shows that of the two-thirds of 18-24s not in full-time education or training, only 73% are in employment). Despite lately resuming what Rikowski (2006) characterised as their 'long moan' about school standards, as the UKCES reports referred to in Chapter Two showed, employers are generally satisfied with the skill levels of the young people they employ, particularly those more highly qualified. The problem is that they just don't employ enough of them. Without a change in the way the economy is organised, young people's chances are not going to be seriously improved, and there will need to be clear policies for improving their position, not only in employment, but also in relation to housing, for instance.

One example of how changes to education and training could combine with economic and statutory measures to rebuild a process of 'youth transition' might be in a real reconstruction of the apprenticeship system, together with a reaffirmation of the original vocational purpose of academic education. Chapter Four demonstrated how the recent attempt to reinvent apprenticeships as an alternative to 'the great university gamble' had largely failed, offering no definite employment route for young people, or in many cases, any significant level of technical training. Instead, promises of 'apprenticeships' are covertly introducing compulsory workfare for non-student youth. But it doesn't have to be like this.

In Germany, rather than just being linked to a specific job or a particular employer for a relatively short period of time, completing an apprenticeship is a civic entitlement that is also considered a rite of passage to employment and adulthood. Compared to their UK counterparts, German apprentices enjoy a high level of education and training, with 90% of apprenticeship starting at level 3 (equivalent to A-level). However, as was noted, the two systems differ in many other ways. (See Allen and Ainley, 2014, in particular the section on 'Why we can't do it like the Germans'). The German apprenticeship system is a product of postwar 'social partnership', a relationship that depends on a strong regulatory framework. Employers and trade unions are both committed to the maintenance of national regulation involving both legislation and high levels of state direction and finance.

German labour markets are closely integrated with national coordination of research and development. All employers with more than 500 employees are required to offer apprenticeships. Apprentices sign a contract lasting for around three years with a company licenced as a provider. Apprenticeships reach well beyond manufacturing – only one in four enter this sector. Providing a 'licence to practice', labour market entrants are only legally permitted to take up many occupations if they have completed an apprenticeship for them. Forty out of every 1,000 employees are apprentices, while a smaller proportion of young Germans attend university than in the UK; 60% of young people complete apprenticeships of several years, and 90% of these then secure employment. German youth unemployment is consistently less than half that in the UK.

The German system is not perfect (see Busemeyer et al, 2012 for reservations), however. German workers have suffered from the same global pressures as the UK, but the apprenticeship system and its ability to provide a meaningful transition for young people is far from anything that has existed for a long time in the UK. As a result, it could not simply be imported, but is cited as an example of the type of integrated industrial and social strategy that would be needed, but which none of the UK austerity parties can remotely conceive of. In the absence of these conditions, trade unions can seek to negotiate as many safeguards as regards training and guarantees of employment on completion as they can into the apprentice agreements that they are party to. At the same time, the TUC can learn the lessons from the 1980s YTS, when many unions were strung along by government and employers into giving credence to increasingly worthless MSC schemes.

Initiatives need to focus on job creation, no longer following the credo of neoliberal human capitalism that 'upskilling' the workforce will magically conjure up new employment opportunities. Repeatedly, 'supply-side' solutions have shown themselves inadequate to challenge the structural (demand-side) weaknesses of the UK's 'declining' – if not 'moribund' – economy. As argued above, the UK lacks anything that resembles an 'industrial strategy', and, ever since the dissolution of the DfE in 1995, has relied on ill-conceived education policies to substitute for one. For example, rather than attempting to mimic aspects of individually competitive and collectively regimented East Asian school systems, it should be recognised that, as in Germany – despite differences in both emphasis and operation – the national state apparatus as much as the market continues to play a leading role in the economy and in education.

## Conclusion

By contrast with Germany, Scotland and other European countries, for the foreseeable future England is stuck with a one-track government that knows only the emergency responses with which Mrs Thatcher postponed the crisis of capital accumulation in the 1970s. Deregulation of all public services with the privatisation of provision on the contracting-out state model is seen by ministers as the solution to every problem, and is part of the motivation for those seeking to leave the 'overly regulated' EU. A small state with 'low welfare' in a free market is the narrow-minded ideal, but it reflects more than poverty of imagination in response to the global challenges that threaten to overwhelm humanity. As Karl Polanyi wrote in tracing the origins of European fascism back to the same neoliberal economic model,

> … the idea of a self-adjusting market implied a stark utopia. Such an institution could not exist for any length of time without annihilating the human and natural substance of society; it would have physically destroyed man and transformed his surroundings into a wilderness. (1944, p 3)

This is the reality that once again confronts society.

As 'the human environment and the natural environment deteriorate together', Pope Francis writes that 'the silent rupture of the bonds of integration and social cohesion… [is a] real social decline' (2015, pp 25-6). Culture – 'the whole expanding corpus of human knowledge [that] must be relearnt about three times in each century' (Vickers, 1965, p 108) – is especially vulnerable because it is a collective creation that is reduced in its theoretical scope and practical applications by the individualised competition now institutionalised in education. Competition does not raise 'standards', save those that can be ranked in numerical order, narrowing performance to what can be assessed in prescribed behaviours. Through largely literary examinations, the education industry functions as a giant sorting machine, rewarding what it recognises as accomplishments of more or less expensively acquired cultural capital. It thus pulls off 'the trick', as Bourdieu and Passeron called it in *The inheritors*, of appearing objective while actually being biased towards the reproduction of privilege.

The magic is waning from this particular trick, just as the gloss is fading from the shiny enticements of educational advertising. The creeping crisis of legitimacy at all levels of learning is manifested in bizarre symptoms of stress for teachers and taught alike. Meanwhile, a near universal cynicism lightens despairing resignation to the rituals of performance. Nevertheless, within the interstices of the system of 'functional stupidity', as Alvesson labels education and the larger commercialised culture with its 'socially supported lack of reflexivity, substantive reasoning, and justification' (2013, p 216), it is still possible to inform resistance with ideas of alternatives. Indeed, as the crisis of legitimacy inflects every aspect of education, human imagination seeks its liberation in the resolution of what is a generational crisis for young people, and therefore for the whole of society and its future.

# References

Ainley, P. (1988) *From school to YTS, education and training in England and Wales 1944-1987*, Milton Keynes: Open University Press.

Ainley, P. (1993) *Class and skill: Changing divisions of knowledge and labour*, London: Cassell.

Ainley, P. (2001) 'From a National System Locally Administered to a National System Nationally Administered: The New Leviathan in Education and Training in England' in *The Journal of Social Policy*, Vol.30, No.3, 2001, pp.457 - 476.

Ainley, P. (2008) *'Twenty years of schooling...' Student reflections on their educational journeys*, London: Society for Research into Higher Education.

Ainley, P. (2013) 'Education and the reconstitution of social class in England', *Research in Post-Compulsory Education*, vol 18, nos 1-2, pp 46-60.

Ainley, P. (2014) 'Follow your dreams and attend university if possible', *Latitude*, University of Greenwich Students' Union magazine, 21 December.

Ainley, P. (2015) 'English higher education: fees are only the half of it!', *Forum*, vol 57, no 1, pp 59-66.

Ainley, P. (2016: forthcoming) 'The business studies university: turning higher education into further education', *The London Review of Education*.

Ainley, P. and Allen, M. (2010) *Lost generation? New strategies for youth and education*, London: Continuum.

Ainley, P. and Bailey, B. (1997) *The business of learning: Staff and student experiences of further education in the 1990s*, London: Cassell.

Ainley, P. and Corney, M. (1990) *Training for the future: The rise and fall of the Manpower Services Commission*, London: Cassell.

Allen, M. (2004) 'The rise and fall of the GNVQ. Young people and vocational qualifications at the start of the twenty-first century', Unpublished PhD thesis, Milton Keynes: Open University.

Allen, M. (2007) 'Learning for labour: specialist diplomas and 14-19 education', *Forum*, vol 49, no 3, pp 7-9.

Allen, M. (2010) 'The new business studies generation', Presentation to the Society for Research into Higher Education, Student Experience Network day event, 'The student experience of business studies', University of Greenwich Business School, 27 January.

Allen, M. (2015) *Hard labour: Young people moving into work in difficult times*, London: Radicaled.

Allen, M. (2016) *Another great training robbery or a real alternative for young people? Apprenticeships at the start of the twenty-first century*, rewritten and updated January 2016, London: Radicaled.

Allen, M. and Ainley, P. (2008a) 'Education and the crunch: gloom and opportunities', in T. Green (ed) *Blair's educational legacy: Thirteen years of New Labour*, Basingstoke: Macmillan.

Allen, M. and Ainley, P. (2008b) *A new 14+: Vocational diplomas and the future of schools, colleges and universities*, Educational and campaigning pamphlet, London: Ealing Teachers' Association with Greenwich University and University and College Union.

Allen, M. and Ainley, P. (2012) 'Running from the riots – up a down-escalator in the middle of a class structure gone pear-shaped', Contribution to 'The riots one year on' conference, 28 September, London: South Bank University.

Allen, M. and Ainley, P. (2013a) *The great reversal: Young people, education and employment in a declining economy*, London: Radicaled.

Allen, M. and Ainley, P. (eds) (2013b) *Education beyond the coalition: Reclaiming the agenda*, London: Radicaled.

Allen, M. and Ainley, P. (2014) *Another great training robbery or a real alternative for young people? Apprenticeships at the start of the 21st century*, London: Radicaled.

Alvesson, M. (2013) *The triumph of emptiness: Consumption, higher education and work organization*, Oxford: Oxford University Press.

Arnold, M. (1939) 'Culture and Anarchy' in *Arnold, Poetry and Prose*, Oxford: Clarendon Press.

Aronowitz, S. (2008) *Against schooling: For an education that matters*, Boulder. CO: Paradigm.

Ashton, D., Maguire, M. and Spilsbury, M. (1990) *Restructuring the labour market: The implications for youth*, London: Macmillan.

Atkinson, J. (1984) *Emerging UK work patterns in flexible manning: The way ahead*, Report 88, Brighton: Institute of Manpower Studies, University of Sussex.

Bailey, M. and Freedman, D. (eds) (2011) *The assault on universities: A manifesto for resistance*, London: Pluto.

Baker, K. (2013) *14-18: A new vision for secondary education*, London: Bloomsbury.

Ball, S. (2012) *Politics and policy making in education: Explorations in sociology*, Report no 33, London: Routledge.

Ball, S. (2015) 'Pearson and PALF', *Education in Crisis* blog, London: Institute of Education, UCL.

Ball, S., Maguire, M. and Macrae, S. (2000) *Choices, pathways and transitions post-16*, London: RoutledgeFalmer.

Beadle, P. (2015) *How to teach literacy*, Carmarthen: Independent Thinking Press.

Becker, G. (1964) *Human capital: A theoretical and empirical analysis with special reference to education*, Chicago, IL: University of Chicago Press.

Bell, D. and Blanchflower, D. (2009) *Youth unemployment: Déjà vu?*, Stirling: Management School, University of Stirling.

Benn, C. and Chitty, C. (1996) *Thirty years on is comprehensive education alive and well or struggling to survive?*, London: Fulton.

Bernstein, B. (1970) 'Education cannot compensate for society', *New Society*, 26 February.

Beynon, H. (1975) *Working for Ford*, Wakefield: EP Publishing.

BHA (British Humanist Association) (2015) *An unholy mess: How virtually all religiously selective state schools in England are breaking the law*, London: BHA.

BIS (Department for Business, Innovation and Skills) (2011) *Higher education: Students at the heart of the system*, London: BIS.

BIS (2013) *The international survey of adult skills 2012: Adult literacy, numeracy and problem solving skills*, London: BIS.

Blenkinsopp, J. and Scurry, T. (2007) 'Hey gringo! The HR challenge of graduates in non-graduate occupations', *Personnel Review*, vol 35, no 4, pp 623-7.

Bourdieu, P. and Passeron, J.-C. (1964) *Les heretiers*, Paris: Editions de Minuit. [Translated by R. Nice, 1972, as *The inheritors: French students and their relation to culture*, Chicago, IL: University of Chicago Press.]

Bowles, S. and Gintis, H. (1976) *Schooling in capitalist America: Educational reform and the contradictions of economic life*, New York: Basic Books.

Braverman, H. (1974) *Labour and monopoly capital: The degradation of work in the twentieth century*, New York: Monthly Review Press.

Brown, P. (1987) *Schooling ordinary kids*, London: Tavistock.

Brown, P. and Lauder, H. (1992) 'Education, economy and society. An introduction to a new agenda', in P. Brown and H. Lauder (eds) *Education fo*

Brown, P., Lauder, H. and Ashton, D. (2011) *The global auction: The broken promise of education, jobs and incomes*, Oxford: Oxford University Press.

Brynjolfsson, E. and McAfee, A. (2014) *The second machine age: Work, progress, and prosperity in a time of brilliant technologies*, New York: Norton.

Busemeyer, M., Neubäumer, R., Pfeifer, H. and Wenzelmann, F. (2012) 'The transformation of the German vocational training regime: evidence from firms' training behaviour', *Industrial Relations Journal*, vol 43, no 6, pp 572-91.

Bynner, J. (2005) *Rethinking the youth phase of the life course: The case for emerging adulthood*, London: Bedford Group for Life Course and Statistical Studies, Institute of Education.

Byrne, L. (2014) *Robbins rebooted: How we earn our way in the second machine age*, London: Social Market Foundation.

Cabinet Office (2009) *New opportunities: Fair chances for the future*, London: The Stationery Office.

CACC (Campaign Against Climate Change) (2010) *One million climate jobs now*, London: CACC.

Callinicos, A. and Harman, C. (1987) *The changing working class*, London: Bookmarks.

Cameron, D. (2015) *A Britain that gives every child the best start in life* posted 2nd February 2015 http://press.conservatives.com/post/109906886845/David-Cameron-a-britain-that-gives-every-child

Castells, M. (2001) 'Information technology and global development' in J. Muller, N. Cloete and S. Badet (eds) *Challenges of Globalisation, South African debates with Manuel Castells*, Capetown: Maskew Miller/ Longmans.

Cheeseman, M. (2011) 'The pleasures of being a student at the University of Sheffield', Unpublished PhD thesis, Sheffield: University of Sheffield.

Chitty, C. (2004) 'Eugenic theories and concepts of ability', in M. Benn and C. Chitty (eds) *A tribute to Caroline Benn, education and democracy*, London: Continuum, pp 76-96.

CIPD (Chartered Institute of Personnel Directors) (2015) *Overqualification and skills-mismatch in the graduate labour market*, London: CIPD.

Clark, T. and Heath, A. (2014) *Hard times: Inequality, recession, aftermath*, London: Yale University Press.

Cohen, P. (1997) *Rethinking the youth question*, Basingstoke: Macmillan.

Collins, H. (2014) *Are we all scientific experts now?*, Cambridge: Polity.

Collins, H. and Evans, R. (2007) *Rethinking expertise*, Chicago, IL: University of Chicago Press.

Cooley, M. (1987) *Architect or bee? The human price of technology*, London: Hogarth.

Coultas, V. (2013) 'English for the few or for the many?', in M. Allen and P. Ainley (eds) *Education beyond the coalition, reclaiming the agenda*, London: Radicaled, pp 46-60.

Cox, E. and Davies, B. (2014) *Driving a generation: Improving the interaction between schools and businesses*, London: Institute for Public Policy Research.

Crompton, R. and Jones, G. (1984) *White-collar proletariat: Deskilling and gender in clerical work*, London: Macmillan.

Davis, A., Hirsch, D. and Padley, M. (2015) *A minimum income standard for the UK in 2014*, York: Joseph Rowntree Trust.

Denham, A. and Garnett, M. (2002) *Keith Joseph*, Brixton: Acumen.

DES (Department of Education and Science) (1965) *The organisation of secondary education*, Circular 10/65, London: HMSO.

DfE (2010) *The importance of teaching, The Schools White Paper 2010*, London: DfE.

DfEE (Department for Education and Employment) (1997) *Excellence in schools*, London: DfEE.

DfES (Department for Education and Skills) (2005) *Higher standards, better schools for all*, London: DfES.

DfES (Department for Education and Skills) (2007) *Raising expectations: Staying in education and training post-16*, London: DfES.

Dorling, D. (2014) *Inequality and the 1%*, London: Verso.

Dorling, D. (2015) 'Money changes everything' in *Times Higher Education*, 12/2/15, pp 36-40.

Drucker, P. (1993) *Post-capitalist society*, Butterworth: Heinemann.

EHRC (Equality and Human Rights Commission) (2015) *Is Britain fairer? The state of equality and human rights 2015*, London: EHRC.

Elias, P. and Purcell, K. (2006) *Futuretrack Survey of the class of 2006 applicants for higher education*, University of Warwick: Institute for Employment Research.

Eliot, T.S. (1963) Choruses from 'The rock', *Collected Poems 1909-1962*, London: Faber.

Equality Trust (2011) *Income inequality: Trends and measures*, London: Equality Trust.

Evans, G. (2006) *Educational failure and working class white children in Britain*, Basingstoke: Basingstoke.

Felstead, A. and Green, F. (2013) *Skills in focus: Underutilisation, overqualification and skills mismatch: Patterns and trends*, Glasgow: Skills Development Scotland.

Ferri, E., Bynner, J. and Wadsworth, M. (eds) (2003) *Changing Britain, changing lives: Three generations at the turn of the century*, Bedford Way Papers, London: Institute of Education.

Finegold, D. and Soskice, D. (1988) 'The failure of training in Britain: analysis and prescription', *Oxford Review of Economic Policy*, vol 4, no 3, pp 21-53.

Finn, D. (1987) *Training without jobs: New deals and broken promises*, London: Macmillan.

Fisher, A. (2014) *The failed experiment and how to build an economy that works*, West Wickham: The Radical Read Project.

Frey, C. and Osborne, M. (2013) *The future of computerisation: How susceptible are jobs to computerisation?*, Oxford: Engineering Sciences Department, University of Oxford.

Glaser, E. (2012) *Get real: How to see through the hype, spin and lies of modern life*, London: Fourth Estate.

Glyn, A. (2006) *Capitalism unleashed*, Oxford: Oxford University Press.

Glyn, A. and Sutcliffe, B. (1972) *British capitalism, workers and the profits squeeze*, Harmondsworth: Penguin.

Goldthorpe, J., Lockwood, D., Bechhofer, F. and Platt, J. (1969) *The affluent worker in the class structure*, Cambridge: Cambridge University Press.

Goos, M. and Manning, A. (2003) *Lousy and lovely jobs: The rising polarization of work in Britain*, London: London School of Economics and Political Science.

Gorz, A. (1980) *Farewell to the working class: An essay on post-industrial socialism*, London: Pluto.

Griffin, C. (1985) *Typical girls*, London: Routledge.

Grubb, N. and Lazerson, M. (2005) 'The education gospel and the role of vocationalism in American education', *American Journal of Education*, vol 111, no 3, pp 297-320.

Hall, S. (2005) 'New Labour's double-shuffle', *Review of Education, Pedagogy, and Cultural Studies*, vol 27, no 4, pp 319-35.

Harbour, C. (2015) *John Dewey and the future of community college education*, London: Bloomsbury.

HMSO (1942) *Social Insurance and Allied Services (The Beveridge Report)*, Cmnd. 6404, London: HMSO.

HMSO (1963) *Half our future, Report of the Central Advisory Council for Education (England)*, London: HMSO.

HMSO (1975) *A Language for Life (The Bullock Report)*, London: HMSO.

Hills, J. (2010) *An anatomy of economic inequality in the UK: Report of the National Equality Panel*, London: The Stationery Office.

Hills, J., Sefton, T. and Stewart, K. (2009) *Towards a more equal society*, Bristol: Policy Press.

Hirsch, E. (2006) *The knowledge deficit: Closing the shocking educational gap for American children*, New York: Houghton Mifflin.

Hobsbawm, E. (1968) *Industry and empire*, London: Pelican.

Hodgson, A. and Spours, K. (2015) 'The future of FE colleges in England: The case for a new post-incorporation model', in A. Hodgson (ed) *The coming of age for FE? Reflections on the past and the future role of further education colleges in England*, London: Institute of Education Press.

Holmwood, J. (ed) (2012) *A manifesto for the public university*, London: Bloomsbury.

Hudson, M. (2014) *Casualisation and low pay: A report for the Trades Union Congress*, London: Trades Union Congress.

Hutchins, M. (2015) *Exam factories?*, London: National Union of Teachers.

Illich, I. (1971) *Deschooling society*, New York: Marion Boyars.

IPSE (The Association of Independent Professionals and the Self Employed) (2014) *Economic outlook: The self-employed perspective*, London: IPSE.

Jeffs, T. and Smith, M. (eds) (1990) *Using informal education*, Buckingham: Open University Press.

Jessup, G. (1991) *Outcomes: NVQs and the emerging model of education and training*, Brighton: Falmer Press.

Johnson, R. (1976) 'Notes on the schooling of the English working class 1780-1850', in R. Dale, G. Esland and M. MacDonald (eds) *Schooling and capitalism: A sociological reader*, London and Milton Keynes: Routledge and Open University Press.

Jones, K. (2003) *Education in Britain: 1944 to the present*, London, Wiley.

Jones, K. (2016) *Education in Britain: 1944 to the present*, second edition, Cambridge: Polity.

Jones, O. (2011) *Chavs: The demonization of the working class*, London: Verso.

Klein, N. (2007) *Shock doctrine: The rise of disaster capitalism*, New York: Picador.

Lansley, S. (2012) *The cost of inequality*, London: Gibson Square.

Lansley, S. and Mack, J. (2015) *Breadline Britain: The rise of mass poverty*, London: Oneworld.

Latham, P. (2011) *The state and local government: Towards a new basis for 'local democracy' and the defeat of big business control*, Croydon: Manifesto Press.

Lave, J. and McDermott, R. (2002) 'Estranged (labor) learning', *Outlines*, vol 1, no 1, pp 19-48.

Leadbeater, C. (2000) *Living on thin air: The new economy*, London: Viking.

Leitch, S. (2006) *Review of skills: Prosperity for all in a global economy*, Norwich: The Stationery Office.

Lethbridge, J. (2015) 'How public management reform influenced three professional groups – teachers, nurses and social workers – in England during the period 1979-2010', Unpublished PhD thesis, London: University of Greenwich.

Lingfield, R. (2012) *Professionalism in FE: Final report of the Independent Review Panel*, London: Department for Business, Innovation and Skills.

Lockwood, D. (1958) *The blackcoated worker*, London: Allen & Unwin.

Martell, G. (1976) 'The politics of reading and writing', in R. Dale, G. Esland and M. MacDonald (eds) *Schooling and capitalism: A sociological reader*, London and Milton Keynes: Routledge and Open University Press.

Marx, K. (1971) *Capital*, vol 1, London: Unwin.

Marx, K. and Engels, F. (1970) 'The communist manifesto', in *Selected works*, London: Lawrence & Wishart.

McArdle-Clinton, D. (2008) *The consumer experience of higher education: The rise of capsule education*, London: Continuum.

McCullough, A. (2015) *More social mobility versus social structural change*, Lincoln: Social Science Centre, Lincoln University.

McGettigan, A. (2013) *The great university gamble: Money, markets and the future of higher education*, London: Pluto.

McGettigan, A. (2015) 'The accelerated level playing field', Blog, Wonkhe, 6 November.

Mizen, P. (2004) *The changing state of youth*, Basingstoke: Macmillan.

Murray, C. (1990) *The emerging British underclass*, London: Institute of Economic Affairs.

Naidoo, R. and Jamieson, I. (2005) 'Empowering participants or corroding learning? Towards a research agenda on the impact of student consumerism in higher education', *Journal of Education Policy*, vol 20, no 3, pp 267-81.

NAO (National Audit Office) (2002) *Individual Learning Accounts: Report by the Comptroller and Auditor General*, London: NAO.

NPI (New Policy Institute) (2015) *Poverty among young people in the UK*, London: NPI.

NUT (National Union of Teachers) (2014) *Stand up for education: A manifesto for our children's education*, London: NUT.

OECD (Organisation for Economic Development and Co-operation) (2015) *Skills outlook 2015*, Paris: OECD.

Offe, C. (1985) *Disorganized capitalism, contemporary transformations of work and politics*, Cambridge, MA: MIT Press.

Ofsted (Office for Standards in Education) (2015) *Apprenticeships: Developing skills for future prosperity*, Manchester: Ofsted.

ONS (Office for National Statistics) (2013) *Graduates in the UK labour market 2013, Full report*, London: ONS.

ONS (2014a) *Self-employed workers in the UK*, London: ONS.

ONS (2014b) *Young people in the labour market, 2014*, London: ONS.

ONS (2015) *Labour Market Bulletin*. London: ONS.

Palfreyman, D. and Tapper, T. (2014) *Reshaping the university: The rise of the regulated market in higher education*, Oxford: Oxford University Press.

Parkin, F. (1972) *Class, inequality and political order*, London: Paladin.

Perlin, R. (2011) *Intern nation: How to earn nothing and learn little in the brave new economy*, London: Verso.

Picketty, T. (2014) *Capital in the twenty-first century*, Cambridge, MA: Harvard University Press.

Playfair, E. (2015) 'The challenge of creating a system', *Education Politics*, vol 125, pp 10-11.

Polanyi, K. (1944) *The great transformation: The political and economic origins of our time*, New York: Beacon Press.

Pope Francis (2015) '"Laudato Si", On care for our common home', Encyclical Letter, Rome: The Vatican.

Postman, N. and Weingartner, C. (1969) *Teaching as a subversive activity*, New York: Dell.

PwC (PricewaterhouseCoopers) (2009) *The future of UK manufacturing*, London: PwC.

Ranciere, J. (2010) 'On ignorant schoolmasters', in C. Bingham and G. Biesta, *Jacques Ranciere: Education, truth, emancipation*, London: Continuum.

Ravitch, D. (2010) *The death and life of the great American school system: How testing and choice are undermining education*, New York: Basic Books.

Richard, D. (2012) *The Richard review of apprenticeships*, London: Department for Business, Innovation and Skills.

Rikowski, G. (2006) 'The long moan of history: employers on school leavers', *The Volumizer*.

Robbins, Lord (1963) *Higher education* (Robbins Report), Cmnd 2154, London: HMSO.

Roberts, K. (2001) *Class in modern Britain*, Basingstoke: Palgrave Macmillan.

Roberts, K. (2010) 'The end of the long baby-boomer generation? If so, what next?', Unpublished paper, Liverpool: Department of Sociology, University of Liverpool.

Roberts, K. (2011) *Class in contemporary Britain*, Basingstoke: Palgrave Macmillan.

Roberts, K., Clark, C., Cook, F. and Semeonoff, E. (1977) *The fragmentary class structure*, London: Heinemann.

Rose, D. and O'Reilly, K. (1997) *Constructing Classes towards a new social classification for the UK*, Swindon: Economic and Social Research Council and Office of National Statistics.

Scott, P. (2013) 'The coalition government's reform of higher education: Policy formation and political process', in C. Callender and P. Scott (eds) *Browne and beyond: Modernizing English higher education*, London: Institute of Education Press.

Scott, P. (2015) 'What is a university?', Talk at the UK premier of the film 'At Berkeley', London: Birkbeck College, 27 February.

Shildrick, T., MacDonald, R., Webster, C. and Garthwaite, K. (2010) *The low-pay, no-pay cycle: Understanding recurrent poverty*, York: Joseph Rowntree Foundation.

Silva, J. (2015) *Coming up short: Working-class adulthood in an age of uncertainty*, Oxford: Oxford University Press.

Silver, R. (2004) '14-19 reform: The challenge to HE', Presentation to Higher Education Policy Institute, House of Commons, 29 June.

Simmons, R. (2014) '"Sorry to have kept you waiting so long, Mr Macfarlane": further education after the coalition', in M. Allen and P. Ainley (eds) *Education beyond the coalition: Reclaiming the agenda*, London: Radicaled, pp 82-105.

Simon, B. (1991) *Education and the Social Order, 1940-1990*, London: Lawrence and Wishart.

Sissons, P. (2011) *The hourglass and the escalator: Labour market change and mobility*, Lancaster: Work Foundation, Lancaster University.

Solomon, C. and Palmieri, T. (eds) (2011) *Springtime: The new student rebellions*, London: Verso.

Snow, C. (1959) *The two cultures and the scientific revolution*, Cambridge: Cambridge University Press.

Spours, K. and Hodgson, A. (2012) *Towards a universal upper secondary education system in England: A unified and ecosystem vision*, London: Institute of Education.

Standing, G. (2011) *The precariat: The new dangerous class*, London: Bloomsbury.

Sweet, S. and Meiksins, P. (2013) *Changing contours of work, jobs and opportunities in the new economy*, London: Sage.

Taylor, F. (1947) *Scientific management*, New York: Harper & Row.

Todd, S. (2014) *The people: The rise and fall of the working class 1910-2010*, London: Murray.

Turner, J. (2015) 'Barely under control. Jenny Turner on the privatisation of schools', *London Review of Books*, vol 37, no 9, pp 6-14.

UKCES (UK Commission for Employment and Skills) (2015) *Skills survey*, London: UKCES.

UNISON (2014) *Stars in our schools: School support staff survey 2014 – Summary of results*, London: UNISON.

University Alliance (2012) *The way we'll work: Labour market trends and preparing for the hourglass*, London: University Alliance.

Vickers, G. (1965) *The art of judgement: A study of policy making*, London: Chapman & Hall.

Waugh, C. (2015) *Class struggle: Adult education for the 21st century*, Draft manifesto for the Independent Working Class Education Network (www.iwceducation.co.uk)

Wilks, S. (2013) *Power, Money but Little Accountability, The rise of the new corporate state*. Manchester Policy Bloggs: Whitehall Watch 8th December http:/blog.policy.manchester.ac.uk/featured/201312?power-money-but-little-accountability-the rise-of-the new-corporate-state/.

Willis, P. (1977) *Learning to labour*, Farnborough: Saxon House.

Wolf, A. (2011) *Review of vocational education* (Wolf Report), London: Department for Education.

Wolf, A. (2015) *Heading for the precipice: Can further and higher education funding policies be sustained?*, London: Policy Institute, King's College London.

Wright, E.O. (1989) *The debate on classes*, London and New York: Verso.

Zuboff, S. (1988) *In the age of the smart machine: The future of work and power*, Oxford: Heinemann.

# Index